Reaching for More

Reaching for More

Pascal Foresi

new city press, new york

First published under the title *Conversazioni con i focolarini*
by Città Nuova Editrice, Rome
translated by Hugh J. Moran
Published in the United States by New City Press
the publishing house of the Focolare Movement, Inc.
206 Skillman Avenue, Brooklyn, N.Y. 11211
© by New City Press, New York

Scripture texts from the New Testament used in this work,
unless otherwise indicated, are taken from
the *New American Bible*, copyright © 1970, by the
Confraternity of Christian Doctrine, Washington, D.C.,
and are used by permission of the copyright owner.
All rights reserved.

Scripture texts from the Old Testament,
unless otherwise indicated, are taken from
The *Revised Standard Version, Common Bible*,
copyright © 1973. Used with permission.

Excerpts from the *Jerusalem Bible*,
copyright © 1966 by Darton, Longman and Todd, Ltd.
and Doubleday & Company, Inc., are
used by permission of the publisher.

Cover design by Nick Cianfarani
Library of Congress Catalog Number: 82-0211
ISBN 0-911782-40-0
Printed in the United States of America

Contents

	Foreword	7
1.	God is love	9
2.	Choosing God	19
3.	The word of life	34
4.	The new commandment	45
5.	Jesus in our midst	55
6.	Jesus forsaken	70
7.	The call to follow Jesus	82
8.	The call to discipleship	96
9.	Faith, hope, and love	113
10.	Wisdom	125
11.	Reaching for more	134
12.	Prayer	147
	Notes	157

Foreword

When the contents of this book were prepared it was not with publication in mind. The various chapters began as informal talks given to groups of friends—members of the Focolare Movement—on various occasions and in different circumstances. The talks were not prepared as a complete series and the present collection does not claim to give an overall picture of a Christian spirituality or way of life. Many topics basic to any Christian movement are not touched on here, but are taken for granted as the necessary background for the subjects which are included.

Although some alterations in form have been made in transcribing this material for publication, the order of the spoken rather than the written word has been preserved. The untechnical language of the original has been kept so that the spiritual content might have a more immediate impact for readers unfamiliar with theological terms.

My hope is that, within its limitations, this book will achieve its intended purpose which is to help its readers toward a deeper understanding of, and a more intimate friendship with, Jesus and the Church which is Christ living in the world today.

P. Foresi

1

GOD IS LOVE

Recently, while meditating on the Scriptures, I was quite struck by a statement in the book of Exodus, which is repeated several times in the description of Moses' relationship with God. Moses, as you know, had an extraordinary contact with God. Yet, although God had revealed himself to him in the form of a burning bush—that is, in a way that could be perceived by his senses—God would not allow Moses to see him face to face.

After many years of such close contact, Moses asked God to be allowed to see him. God replied:

> You cannot see my face; for man shall not see me and live. Behold, there is a place by me where you shall stand upon the rock; and while my glory passes by I will put you in a cleft of the rock, and I will cover you with my hand until I have passed by; then I will take away my hand, and you shall see my back; but my face shall not be seen (Ex. 33:20-23).

Since the whole of the Old Testament looks forward to Christ, this incident sheds a completely new light on Christian death, giving it a special significance: death allows us to see God. It is no longer a sign of sin and punishment; God's mercy has transformed it into a sign of his greatest love.

Our entire life should be rooted in this certainty: it is not so much that what is negative can be made to serve a positive end, as that the positive itself which God wills for us—the love he wishes to give us—sometimes requires the negative.

Therefore, as we have often heard, rather than stress the renunciation in Christian life, we should focus our attention on becoming filled with God. This attitude is of great value in the spiritual life, as each of us has undoubtedly experienced.

Yes, death, suffering, and pain are certainly demanded as part of the Christian life; but only because the positive—God's love—is there to illuminate each dark moment and give meaning to everything. That is why I would like to meditate with you on God's love. We are so immersed in the Christian life, as something perfectly normal, that we frequently forget how great his love for us really is.

Not long ago I visited a country where atheism predominates and, although my stay was brief, I was deeply saddened by what I saw there. How many problems trouble the hearts of those people! They must have at least all the spiritual difficulties that Christians experience. And if they drift away from God and undergo moral or spiritual crises, they have no sure way of knowing how to regain inner peace and contact with God. They have to deal with all their problems almost entirely on their own, or at least without as much light as Christians have. Consider, for example, how fortunate we are to have the sacrament of reconciliation. For besides acting as God's representative in absolving us from our sins, a confessor also gives us advice and enlightens us, often indicating whether a given act is good or not. If we are seeking the truth we are happy to have someone point out to us the errors we have made, and this awareness of our mistakes prompts us to ask God's forgiveness for all that has happened and to abandon ourselves to his mercy. And this in turn makes life itself more meaningful.

There are many people living outside Christianity who will never be able to find a sure answer regarding the moral significance of certain acts or situations. Take divorce, for example: is it something good or something harmful?

How many problems these people and their children will have, simply because they were not born thirty miles away in a place where there was a Christian community!

Generally speaking, most of us live in a Christian setting; we were born into Christian families and raised in a Christian environment. In this way, each of us has assimilated many Christian principles, many things which are good, pure, and holy. Yet so often we forget that this is so only because God has had a special love for each one of us. Of course, this brings with it certain responsibilities, but we want to focus primarily upon the fact that all this is a gift from God.

How immense God's love for us must be, if out of hundreds of millions of people he has chosen to share his good news with us!

God must certainly love you and me personally, since he has made us Christians and helped us to grasp something of his marvelous revelation, thereby enabling us to overcome life's greatest difficulties. Moreover, he has also bestowed another enormous grace on us by giving us a clearer insight into the essence of Christianity. Here, I am not yet referring to the vocation to give oneself to God, which is a further gift of his personal love. To understand my point, let each of us think back on his or her spiritual state prior to discovering that God is love. We may have been good; we may have been bad—but that is still not what I am concerned with now. Rather, what I mean is this: how did we understand Christianity? How did we perceive religion, union with God, and all those wonderful gifts of his which are the only things capable of nourishing our souls?

Just think what a special gift it was to discover the beauty of Christian unity! For it is possible to be a person of great generosity, to live a life of self-denial and fervent piety, and yet not come to the realization that the essence of Christianity is love. Therefore, one of the themes that should permeate our meditation is gratitude to God for the gifts he has given us. He has called us out of many backgrounds and countries, from amidst the most diverse peoples and situations. He has focused his personal attention on each of us.

Perhaps we ought to reflect on the fact that God is not an impersonal entity or some sort of corporation, even if we often believe him to be so far off, in a world so different from ours, that he becomes something abstract. At such times we overlook the fact that Jesus is a person and that his love is extremely personal.

One reason we fall into this mistaken view of God is that although we believe that God is three persons, this Trinity seems so mysterious and so far removed from us that, instead of recognizing in the Trinity the absolute fullness of the beauty we find in human personality, we act almost as if this were totally lacking in the divine persons. A second reason is that, not having much experience of God, we relegate him to a sphere somewhere outside ourselves, whereas we should be making the effort to realize that we have always been surrounded by his love. God has taken a personal interest in each of us, and therefore our relationship with him must be personal.

In addition to helping us know him more fully, God has given us a vocation to follow him in a life of apostolate. This, too, is an immense gift; it is what the Gospel story of the rich young man is referring to when it says: "Jesus looked at him and loved him" (Mk. 10:21).

At a given moment in the life of each of us God looked at us and brought us to the understanding of Christianity. Then, looking at us again, he called us to his service. No, not merely to his service—he called us to himself, he wanted us to be his.

In calling us, Jesus has not emphasized that we are called *to his service*, but rather he has loved us so that he might possess us and be possessed by us; so that we might give ourselves totally to him and he might be able to give himself totally to us. This is the essence of his call.

If we make a complete gift of ourselves to him as he has to us, we will obviously be giving up certain other things as a consequence. This renunciation is an intrinsic part of Jesus' call. Thus if I give myself totally to Jesus, it is clear that I will not cling to the passing goods of this earth. In this way poverty, which in itself could be considered a form of renunciation, becomes something positive because God has revealed to us the great wealth that he himself is, and the emptiness of all that the world regards as riches. Gospel poverty, therefore, is born not of a denial but of an affirmation.

The same with purity: God calls us to possess him totally and to be in turn possessed by him. So it is obvious that if we desire God we will not desire anyone else. When we have God revealing himself to us, whatever else we give up is nothing by comparison!

Just think of the gift we are receiving! It is a personal relationship with Jesus—not a relationship between Jesus and millions of people, but between Jesus and each of us.

Just as we are inclined to make God an abstraction, in the same way we are inclined to imagine his love as being parceled out. When we say, "God loves us," our human experience in loving leads us to think of God's love as divided into many parts. We know his love is infinite, but we unconsciously imagine it as divided up among all those he loves. Yet the truth is that his love is infinite for each and every person.

No one can say, "God doesn't love me quite as much as he loves others," because God loves each person with an infinite, all-encompassing love. This is another mystery.

At this point, let us consider how some common obstacles to our understanding of God's love can be overcome. Perhaps in our own lives we have felt something of God's love for us, and have even experienced something of the spiritual life. But we may also have made mistakes in our past life—or even recently. Perhaps even after giving ourselves to God we have not responded fully to the graces he has given us. This being the case, we may be tempted to think: "God would like to love me, but the way I am he couldn't possibly love me."

But *God loves me in a special way just because of the way I am!* Herein lies the mystery. He himself revealed it in the Gospel: "I came not to call the righteous, but sinners" (Mk. 2:17 RSV). Certainly, we all know this, but as an abstract truth, whereas it is vitally important for each of our lives. I must not think that God loves me less because I have not responded to his love, because I have been a sinner, because I am not generous, or because I have not done this or that. We must not project onto God the feelings we have about ourselves.

God loves us infinitely, he loves us personally, even though we are the way we are. Indeed, our being this way makes his love even more evident.

His heart is ablaze with love. He understands us with all our changing moods, our weaknesses, our sins, our failings. He loves us totally, infinitely.

Sometimes we become discouraged in our spiritual life; but there are really no grounds for such discouragement, since God has revealed that he loves each of us personally.

It may happen at times that those around us, those closest to us, do not esteem us, do not appreciate us, or do not love us. At such times we may be tempted to think that this is a reflection of how God feels about us. But this is absolutely untrue. God's love differs from human love, and he loves each of us, even if the world thinks little of us.

We must come to the awareness that God's love for each of us is personal and—if I may use the term—exclusive. He loves me even if I am wicked. He loves me no matter what, even if everyone else despises me. God loves me just because he loves me.

Moreover, although human love does not always affect the person loved, God's love is constantly active in my soul, transforming it and showering it with graces.

Someone might be tempted to think that in order to be loved by God, one must do great things. But great works in and of themselves are of little importance; their worth comes from the love with which they are done.

All the circumstances in our lives, all our failures and successes, are utilized by God as channels of his love.

Some day this love will have become so great, so "possessive," that we will die. This is what Christian death should signify: that God has "tired" of possessing us partially, and so he has taken us to himself.

The world will say that we are dead. But this is not death as the world understands death. It is God bringing us to be with him. The death of those who give themselves to God and live in him should be like Mary's. Her passing from this earth to heaven occurred because God wanted her with him, and so he took her, body and soul. We should live out our lives striving constantly to possess God more fully, until we reach the happy moment of death, which will be the most beautiful moment of our life.

I hope that from now on all of us will always be happy, precisely because God loves us—whether we are good or bad. And if, by chance, one of you is so disheartened as to think, "It is impossible for God to love me," then you, among all of us, are loved in a special way. All you have to do is give yourself to God, with all your failings. At this moment God loves you most especially. He understands you, he knows all about you. He even knows what you yourself do not know—perhaps you are quite different from what you think!

Perhaps some may feel they are mediocre because they have failed to respond generously to God's love. But God also has a special love for these, even if on many occasions they certainly could have done better. He has allowed their faults in order to let them see that they were not loving.

What God wants of us is not so much that we be perfect in outward things, as that we love him completely, totally, exclusively.

That is why it has been revealed to us that "God is love" (1 Jn. 4:16); and love means: God loves *us*; God loves *me*.

2

CHOOSING GOD

On one occasion when a great crowd was with him, [Jesus] turned to them and said, "If anyone comes to me without turning his back on his father and mother, his wife and his children, his brothers and sisters, indeed his very self, he cannot be my follower. Anyone who does not take up his cross and follow me cannot be my disciple. If one of you decides to build a tower, will he not first sit down and calculate the outlay to see if he has enough money to complete the project? He will do that for fear of laying the foundation and then not being able to complete the work; for all who saw it would jeer at him, saying, 'That man began to build what he could not finish.'

"Or if a king is about to march on another king to do battle with him, will he not sit down first and consider whether, with ten thousand men, he can withstand an enemy coming against him with twenty thousand? If he cannot, he will send a delegation while the enemy is still at a distance, asking for terms of peace. In the same way, none of you can be my disciple if he does not renounce all his possessions. Salt is good, but if salt loses its flavor what good is it for seasoning? It is fit for neither the soil nor the manure heap; it has to be thrown away. Let him who hears this, heed it" (Lk. 14:25-35).

Jesus addressed these words to a huge crowd of people who were following him, fascinated by his words and his miracles, particularly the multiplication of the loaves. Thus these words are meant for everyone—lay people and clergy alike, those who are called to married life and those who are called to celibacy. In addressing this crowd, Jesus made clear the conditions that are necessary if we are to call ourselves his disciples.

The first thing he asks of us is very demanding, in fact it seems impossible: "If anyone comes to me without turning his back on [or, as sometimes translated, "hating"] his father and mother, his wife and his children, his brothers and sisters, indeed his very self, he cannot be my follower." The words "turn his back on," "hate," are certainly not to be understood here as they are used in our current, everyday language. For in Hebrew and Aramaic, shades of meaning that we would normally express by using a variety of verbs, such as "to love," "to love intensely," "to hate," "to be estranged," "to love less than," etc., are often simplified and expressed by a single verb indicating aversion or affection. This is done in order to highlight the contrast. Certainly, Jesus, who taught us to love even our enemies, could not have taught us to hate the members of our own family.[1]

The fact is, "Jesus desires interior allegiance to his person and his teaching, and such allegiance is impossible without renunciation. . . . The family can be an obstacle to doing God's will. If so, it is necessary to "hate" the family by putting God above everything else, whatever it may cost our nature. This is not the feeling of hatred, but an attitude which puts love of Christ above legitimate family affections."[2] That is why in Matthew's Gospel we find, "Whoever loves father or mother, son or daughter, more than me is not worthy of me" (10:37), words emphasizing the priority that must be given to love for Christ.

Jesus specifically mentions all family affections: love of father, mother, spouse, children, brothers and sisters. No human love is excluded. By using these examples, Jesus wants to place before us all the strongest earthly loves.

The necessity of renouncing these loves becomes very clear in cases where one is forced to choose between faith in Christ and love for the members of one's family. During the persecutions which marked the first few centuries of Christianity, mothers and fathers who chose God had to be ready to die or to see their loved ones die. Nor are such situations merely a thing of the past. In our own day, too, we are forced at times to choose between a life lived according to our faith, and our career or the future of our children. And when such moments come we must know how to make the right choice—or rather, we must have already chosen God in our day-to-day lives if we are to be able to make the right choice in that moment.

Family life itself can often become an obstacle to the life of grace if marriage is not lived as a sacrament, if the special graces it provides for the welfare of the Church and for the birth of new members into the Mystical Body are not taken advantage of.

Even when the couple are striving to live a Christian family life, there can still be the danger that they will limit their vision of the Christian life to the small everyday world in which they live. For in recent years, we have become so concerned with the threats to family unity and stability presented by our society and its laws, that we may easily overlook another real danger facing Christian couples: that of placing the family at the center of all our affections and concerns—almost giving it the place of God in our lives. St. Paul, in the seventh chapter of his first letter to the Corinthians, clearly puts us on our guard against this danger of allowing Christian married love to become a purely natural love: "The married man is busy with this world's demands and occupied with pleasing his wife. This means he is divided" (1 Cor. 7:33-34). If the couple do not place God before even their own affection for one another, they run the risk "of forgetting, in practice, that one must give one's undivided heart to God, and that every other love, every activity for the good of other persons must be penetrated, molded by this essential Love."[3] Therefore, even within the context of the family, total adherence to

Jesus must come before everything else. And this is not simply an invitation, or a piece of advice which one may follow or not as one pleases. It is a prerequisite for being his disciple.

If we do not live this way, we may still not commit serious sins; but can we call ourselves Christians, persons imbued with the doctrine of Christ, simply because we try to avoid serious sin? On the contrary, wouldn't that be a hypocritical and superficial view of Christianity, which is above all a religion of the Spirit? Though we might never commit a serious sin, we would certainly not be fulfilling God's will in its entirety. Moreover, we would be running the risk of seriously offending him, since life is full of difficulties; and sooner or later we will be forced to be honest with ourselves and to say whether we are living for God or catering to our own whims and feelings.

After this initial demand, Jesus makes another: that we deny ourselves. "Anyone who does not take up his cross and follow me cannot be my disciple." He gives us a very concrete image to describe how he wants us to put him ahead of ourselves. He wants to tell us in no uncertain terms what wanting to follow him involves.

Nowadays the word "cross" has become a generic term and lost its original meaning. We could almost say that it has been worn out through overuse, even though it still has the connotation of suffering, pain, misfortune, and so on. However, when Jesus said that we cannot be his disciples unless we take up our cross and follow him, he meant something much more drastic and terrifying. The cross was a frequently-used instrument of Roman punishment, and not many years before Jesus spoke these words, the people of Palestine had seen 2,000 rebels led out to be executed, carrying their crosses. The cross meant the death sentence; it meant all the shame that the one condemned experienced as he was led through the city, carrying his cross on his shoulder as a warning to the people.

In order to illustrate for us what our human nature and our ego will have to face, Jesus chooses this image, which will soon reach its sublime fulfillment in his own crucifixion, and will thus become the very symbol and reality of the Redemption. The Christian who puts himself or herself aside and chooses God is considered strange by those who reason according to the world's mentality, and he or she becomes the object of their ridicule and hostility. With this image, we can see even more clearly the contrast between the Christian and the world: in the eyes of the world, the Christian is a person condemned to death.

But without this denial of self, we cannot be Jesus' disciples.

Finally, Jesus makes a third demand, which is implicit in the first two, but which Luke wants to spell out for us: "In the same way, none of you can be my disciple if he does not renounce all his possessions." "Possessions" indicates not only material goods, but also prestige, power, talents, intelligence, and so on.

Jesus asks all Christians to be detached from their possessions; however he does not ask that everyone demonstrate this detachment in an outward way by living in complete poverty. The Gospel, in fact, tells us that even the rich can be Christians: "When evening fell, a wealthy man from Arimathea arrived, Joseph by name. He was another of Jesus' disciples" (Mt. 27:57).

The rich, however, must become spiritually poor: "Blessed are the poor in spirit, for theirs is the kingdom of heaven" (Mt. 5:3 RSV). Those who do not, run the terrible risk of being damned forever: "It is easier for a camel to pass through a needle's eye than for a rich man to enter the kingdom of God" (Mt. 19:24).

This detachment from possessions which Jesus asks of us all is one of the fundamental points of his teaching, and yet it is one of the areas in which our own Christian life leaves most to be desired. Consequently, we hardly ever hear people speak of Christian poverty—a poverty which is visible in those who consecrate their lives to God, but which should be lived in a spiritual way by all Christians.

Nowadays there is an emphasis on social justice, and rightly so, but frequently it is forgotten that true social justice is a consequence of the spirit of Christian poverty, and that this spirit of poverty is demanded of all, rich and poor alike.

You might ask how one who is rich can ever say in conscience that he or she is spiritually poor. The in-depth consideration that this question requires is not possible here, but the following points may shed some light on the subject. First: one who is rich must look upon himself or herself not so much as the owner of the goods he or she possesses, but rather as their administrator, since these goods belong first of all to God. Augustine makes this very clear: "'All that you do not possess is mine,' says the Lord. 'And all that you do possess is mine.'"[4] "'Mine,' says God, 'is the gold and the silver; not yours, O rich of the earth.'"[5]

Therefore, a rich person must utilize his or her possessions in a way that is designed to contribute to the good of the whole community.

> Since the right to private property is subordinate to the fundamental right of all persons to enjoy the goods of the earth, we can legitimately conclude that the social dimension of the right to private property is not only an extension of the personal dimension, but dominates and transcends it.
>
> From this it follows that an owner is not acting in accord with the moral law if he or she administers his or her possessions in a selfish manner and then distributes what is left over.[6]

Although the rich remain in possession of their goods, in using them, they must take into account the good of society. Moreover, in their personal lives, rich Christians should be not wasteful but thrifty and honest. As St. Basil says, "If each person took only what was necessary to meet his or her needs and left the rest to the poor, no one would be rich and no one would be poor."[7]

Finally, the surplus of the rich should serve the needs of the poor, as Pope Leo XIII says in his encyclical *Quod apostolici muneris:*

> [The Church] places the rich under grave obligation to give their surplus goods to the poor, and she puts fear into their hearts by threatening them with divine judgment; for if they do not come to the aid of those in need, they will be punished with eternal torment.[8]

The possible applications of these principles are too numerous to be dealt with here, but certainly any proposed application must reflect the spirit of the Gospel, which itself is already quite eloquent: "Blessed are the poor in spirit, for theirs is the Kingdom of Heaven." "It is easier for a camel to pass through a needle's eye than for a rich man to enter the kingdom of God." "In the same way, none of you can be my disciple if he does not renounce all his possessions." Any application of these principles that nullifies Jesus' words is most certainly mistaken.

Luke is not satisfied, however, with merely having set down what Jesus asks of us. He also includes the examples Jesus used to illustrate how we can build up the Christian life within us.

Jesus first compares the spiritual life to a tower: "If one of you decides to build a tower, will he not first sit down and calculate the outlay to see if he has enough money to complete the project?" He is telling us that if we want to complete the work we have undertaken, if we want our "new self"[9] to develop harmoniously and to reach the full maturity of Christ within us, then we must consciously and decisively direct our lives toward God. Otherwise our spiritual growth will be stunted, we will grind to a halt, and all who see us will laugh us to scorn.

We Christians must honestly admit that we often appear to others as incomplete human beings. It almost seems that those who have not based their lives on supernatural principles are better-balanced persons. This is because our way of living Christianity is incomplete, and thus the distorted image of Christianity we present to others becomes a cause of scandal and an object of ridicule. Examples of this are the various forms of legalism and hypocrisy, as well as that form of scrupulosity which is very concerned about unimportant matters and yet unconcerned or downright lax about what is important: being scrupulously faithful regarding certain pious practices, for example, and at the same time being uncharitable toward one's neighbors, treating them unjustly, or slandering them.

Such instances seem to fit the example of the unfinished tower quite well. The spirituality behind

CHOOSING GOD 29

them is stunted, because it was not based on a deliberate choice of God.

Jesus presents us with another image as well: that of the king who decides to wage war against another king, without having first counted his own soldiers to see if he has sufficient forces. No sooner has he set out than he is forced to send envoys to offer his surrender and to arrange for a peaceful settlement.

Isn't this image very much like the situation of those Christians who set out to fight against the world for the cause of Christ, but who gradually surrender and reach a compromise with the world's mentality?

The Church's predicament consists precisely in this: that it is in the midst of the world and, therefore, there is always a possibility that the "human" mentality of the world may creep in, penetrating even the holiest and most Christian environments and church associations, even communities of priests and religious.

The spirit of the world is particularly damaging to Christians aiming at perfection, precisely because of the ease with which it insinuates itself into fervent people, because of the secret complicity that it finds in them. In a way it is more damaging than obvious temptations like those to anger and impurity. More than anything else, this natural, human, earthly spirit is what helps to keep people in a state of mediocrity. It breaks and paralyzes their impetus towards the fullness of the love of God, weakening the spirit of faith, the truly supernatural spirit. It drives people to rely on human means and earthly supports, nourishing those subtle forms of self-love which arrest the growth of charity and prevent true interior freedom, true detachment from created things.[10]

This compromise in the souls of one or more people can spread and become a general state of affairs, a collective compromise, which is fertile ground for all sorts of intellectual and moral errors. Note, for example, how the pagan spirit of the Renaissance fostered errors and heresies even worse than itself.

It is like the compromise of the two kings. The Christian, who shares in the kingship of Christ, stoops to come to terms with the Prince of this world by accepting some of the world's ways. For a time the Christian vocabulary will remain, but gradually it will become empty and meaningless. We can easily verify this by looking at how some typically Christian terms have been so distorted through the centuries, that they now have almost the opposite of their original meanings. Take "charity": today it is contrasted with "justice" and identified with almsgiving, whereas it is actually at the heart of every Christian virtue, including justice. How often we hear expressions to this effect: "If we base things on charity instead of on justice, where will we end up?" Such an expression is a clear sign that the speaker is ignorant of the essence of the principal Christian virtue, identifying it with a kind feeling, a polite manner, or material assistance, instead of realizing that charity itself gives life to all the other virtues, including faith.[11]

This change in the meaning of such an important word can only be the result of the compromises which have drained the life out of so many Christians.

It would be interesting to make a study of today's Christian vocabulary in order to see how far our Christian society is from Christ.

The final image we find in this particular passage from Luke is that of salt. Christians are the salt of the earth, the soul of the world. They are spread throughout the population of the world as its leaven. They are indistinguishable from others and yet they are completely different, as illustrated by the unknown, third-century author of the *Letter to Diognetus:*

> Christians are not different from other people in nationality, speech, or customs; they do not live in cities of their own, nor do they use a special language or adopt a peculiar way of life. The doctrine they profess is not a discovery of human ingenuity or active minds. Nor do they support a particular school of human thought as some people do. Whether their lot has been to live in a Greek or foreign city, they follow local custom in the matter of dress, food, and other aspects of daily living; yet they have a common lifestyle which is remarkable and, it must be admitted, extraordinary. They live in their respective countries, but as though they were aliens. They share in all

duties like citizens and suffer all hardships like foreigners. Every foreign land is for them a homeland, and every homeland a foreign land. They marry like everyone else and have children, but they do not abandon the babies that are born. They share a common table, but not a common bed. Though living in the flesh, they do not live according to the flesh. They dwell on earth, but they are citizens of heaven. They obey the established laws, but in their private lives are better than the laws. They love all, but are persecuted by all. They are unknown, and yet they are condemned. They are put to death, yet are more alive than ever. They are poor, but they enrich many. They lack all things, and yet in all things they abound. They are dishonored, yet glory in their dishonor. They are maligned, and yet are vindicated. They are reviled, and yet they bless. They suffer insult, yet they pay respect. They do good, yet are punished with the wicked. When they are punished, they rejoice as though they were getting more out of life. They are assailed by the Jews as Gentiles and are persecuted by the Greeks, yet those who hate them can give no reason for their hatred. In a word, what the soul is to the body Christians are to the world. The soul is diffused in every member of the body, and Christians are scattered in every city in the world. The soul dwells in the body, and yet it is not of the body. So, Christians live in the world, but they are not of the world.[12]

A Christian who is not the soul of the world, who is not the salt of the earth, is nothing. Jesus could have used other terms of comparison; he could have compared Christians to water, trees, or stones. But he wanted to choose that particular substance whose usefulness—whose very identity as it were—is linked to a particular characteristic, without which it is of no use, even as fertilizer. Such is not the case with water, wood, or stone.

The Christian's characteristic vocation is to live the very life of God, to belong to another world. This vocation is not reserved for a few, nor is it the exclusive possession of a particular movement within the Church. It is intended for everyone. All people—each within the context of his or her individual vocation—must rediscover God and choose him anew in each day, each hour, each action of their lives.

3

THE WORD OF LIFE

The following well-known passage from Paul's second letter to Timothy contains much of what can be said about Sacred Scripture:

> All scripture is inspired by God and can profitably be used for teaching, for refuting error, for guiding people's lives and teaching them to be holy. This is how the man who is dedicated to God becomes fully equipped and ready for any good work (2 Tim. 3:16-17 JER).

All Christians believe that God is the author of Sacred Scripture. But often this truth has been reflected upon only theoretically, with various attempts being made to explain the nature and essence of inspiration. What we will do is take a closer look at the reality upon which all agree: that the Scriptures have God as their author. Of course, we must keep in mind that the Scriptures also have human writers as their authors, and this entails a variety of practical and theological consequences which I will mention briefly.

First of all, the sacred writers brought with them to their task their intelligence, their will, and whatever learning and experience of their own culture they possessed. These were their contributions to their writing. They may also have consulted other written documents and borrowed from other religious or secular sources, some of which may even have contained errors, which, however, were eliminated by the sacred writers.

But these writers wrote what they wrote because God inspired them to do so and helped, sustained, and enlightened them. Thus the Sacred Scriptures have two authors: God and the sacred writers. Because of this we cannot expect divine perfection in everything we find written in the Old and New Testaments. For in order to speak to us human beings, God had to use human language; he had to make use of other human beings, who were subject to all the limitations imposed upon them by human nature and by the culture and the times in which they lived. Consequently, in the Bible we find noticeable differences from book to book, and we can see reflections of each writer's limited forms of expression and way of thinking.

That is why Vatican II, in its *Constitution on Divine Revelation*,[13] points out the necessity of studying the Scriptures scientifically, and of understanding how people lived at the times of the various writers, how they thought, and what they meant by certain expressions. The literary forms we find in the Bible must be properly understood if we are to discover what God wants to tell us.

What I have said thus far concerns the human element in Scripture, that which derives from its human authorship. But since God is also its author, Scripture is free of every kind of error—theological, doctrinal, moral, historical—*insofar as the truth conveyed affects our salvation.*

These are the basic points that we must keep in mind as we meditate on the Scriptures.

God is the author of Scripture. This statement immediately takes us far beyond the realm of pure speculative theology. What is an author? If we think of a creative genius, whether novelist, musician, or poet, we observe that through his or her artistic works he or she communicates truth, a facet of human nature, a concrete aspect of human life.

We have all experienced in reading great literary works that even though the outward form may be imperfect, one-sided, or difficult, the author has still been able to communicate to us a basic intuition about human nature, about reality. Moreover, through his or her work we have encountered not only the author's ideas, but the author as well, his or her genius and mind. Similarly, through the Scriptures we come in contact not only with their secondary author, the human writer, but also with their primary author: God.

God speaks to us in human ways; he could not have done otherwise, or we would not have been able to understand him. But through Sacred Scripture—God's literary masterpiece—we reach God. This is stupendous! The Scriptures are not merely a means of transmitting dogmatic truths for us to believe and for theologians to speculate about; they also give us God himself, bringing us into direct contact with him. Vatican II affirms this, declaring that "the Church has always venerated the divine Scriptures just as she venerates the body of the Lord, since from the table of both the word of God and of the body of Christ she unceasingly receives and offers to the faithful the bread of life, especially in the sacred liturgy."[14] This is one effect of God's authorship of Scripture.

Another effect is that the content of Sacred Scripture is true; not only because it is without error (which would be merely a negative affirmation), but because through its words, however unsophisticated or concise, God is telling us the truth about how things really are. We find in Scripture not an absence of error, but a fullness of truth.

Here is an example. In Luke's Gospel Mary is described with the Greek work *kecharitōmenē* which we translate as "full of grace." However, if we study the etymology of *kecharitōmenē*, we discover that it can have many meanings, including "beloved of God" and "full of grace." But the word in itself does not immediately indicate these specific meanings. God chose this word, so rich in meaning, to express for us, in the way and to the extent that was possible at that time, the many treasures he had placed in Mary. He used a word which of itself could have many meanings to express the one idea he had in mind: Mary.

Out of all the possible translations of *kecharitō-*

38 REACHING FOR MORE

menē, the Church accepted "full of grace" (found in the Vulgate), thereby expressing its belief that this was God's intended meaning. And since it was God present in the Church who was interpreting himself in his word, this interpretation is true.

Accordingly, when Pope Pius IX proclaimed the dogma of the Immaculate Conception on December 8, 1854, he referred to the teachings of the Fathers of the Church, who considered that one of the places in Scripture where this truth is contained is that very word, *kecharitōmenē*, spoken to Mary by the angel.

God speaks to us through Scripture, therefore, and he communicates truth to us: truth that is much more than an absence of error, truth that we come to understand more and more fully with the passage of time.

In the word *kecharitōmenē* we can even glimpse a foreshadowing of Mary's assumption, since "full of grace" tells us how much Mary was loved by God, and certainly this love was to be the reason for her assumption into heaven.

Because Scripture contains the truth, it is a most precious treasure. It puts us in contact with God, its author. In it we find the living word, the word of life. But how can we be sure of understanding what the Scriptures contain? The answer is given to us by the Second Vatican Council when it speaks of the Church's patrimony of Divine Revelation, which includes both Scripture and Tradition.

For there is a growth in the understanding of the realities and the words which have been handed down. This happens through the contemplation and study made by believers who treasure these things in their hearts (cf. Lk. 2:19, 51), through the intimate understanding of spiritual things they experience, and through the preaching of those who have received through episcopal succession the sure gift of truth. For, as the centuries succeed one another, the Church constantly moves forward toward the fulness of divine truth until the words of God reach their complete fulfillment in her.[15]

This, then, is how the revelation contained in Sacred Scripture is increasingly understood by the Church down through the centuries. The Council urges the faithful—not only theologians, but all the faithful—to study and meditate on the Scriptures. By such study and meditation they will add to the Church's understanding of the wealth that the Scriptures contain, and they will thereby increase the Church's patrimony.

A second way that the patrimony of the Church is enriched is through the experience which comes from a deeper understanding of spiritual things. This affirmation by the Council clearly indicates that the lives of the saints (that is, lives of union with God and knowledge of the things of God) increase the Church's understanding of Sacred Scripture and, consequently, the Church's heritage. This point is very important, because it shows that the life of each and every Christian can make a constructive contribution to the good of the whole Mystical Body.

Yet another way that this patrimony grows is through the preaching of the bishops. Their task is not merely to study, but to preach. Those in the episcopate have the charism of the truth, which includes the charism to safeguard, preserve, and confirm this truth. Since God has given them the duty of preaching, he has also given them the gift of understanding what must be said.

These, therefore, are the ways indicated by the Council for reaching a greater understanding of the Scriptures.

Christ has revealed himself; the episcopate has the task of safeguarding this truth and passing it on. Yet it is the whole Church which must develop the understanding of this truth, under the guidance and supervision of the episcopate. From these words alone one can see the importance and significance of the Council decrees for laity and clergy alike.

However, we have not yet said all that should be said about the Scriptures. We often point out that we should live the "word of life," and that every passage of Sacred Scripture which expresses a revealed truth given to us by God, in some way puts us in touch with the whole of revealed truth. This is so because each revealed truth brings us into contact with God, the source of all revelation. Thus, when we live a particular word of life we come in contact with God and with all truth. This idea is affirmed by the Scriptures themselves with the words: "All scripture is inspired by God." The Greek word *pasa* ("all") can be interpreted as meaning not only "all," but "every"; that is, "Every passage of scripture is inspired by God and can be profitably used for teaching, for refuting error."

The *Constitution on Divine Revelation*[16] cites the following Scripture passage:

> Indeed, God's word is living and effective, sharper than any two-edged sword. It penetrates and divides soul and spirit, joints and marrow; it judges the reflections and thoughts of the heart. Nothing is concealed from him; all lies bare and exposed to the eyes of him to whom we must render an account (Heb. 4:12-13).

"God's word is living": Sacred Scripture is alive. It is not only the word of life, it is alive, in that through the human words of its secondary authors it places us in contact with its primary author, God. And God is alive, *the* Living One. If Scripture is alive, it is at once life-bearing and life-giving: it brings and gives us life.

So when we approach the Scriptures we encounter God who gives us the life which his inspired words contain.

Hence we can understand the importance of inspiration, which is not a past event, over and done with, but a reality which even today continues to produce effects. "Thus," says Vatican II, "God, who spoke of old, uninterruptedly converses with the Bride of His beloved Son."[17] The process of revelation is finished, but the living God continues to speak to us through the Scriptures.

The word of God is "effective." Generally, when Scripture says God is speaking, it means God is acting. For example: "God said, 'Let there be light'" (Gen. 1:3). What is Scripture telling us here? That God created light. This is the meaning of "God said."

In the same way, the word of God—of God who is the Word—is God in action. Therefore, to say that the word speaks to us, is to say that the word transforms us.

The word of God "penetrates" us; that is, it not only touches our mind, but, through our mind, it affects our whole being. And here the author of the Letter to the Hebrews goes on to explain that God's word comes into our soul—the part of us that is spirit, intellect—and into our body, as well. Through the soul it reaches the whole person.

This is the true character of Sacred Scripture. It is not merely a book to be studied, or in which to find evidence for doctrines which can then be collected into manuals of theology. No, Scripture embraces the whole human person, nourishing us both spiritually—in all that regards our union with God, the apex of the spiritual life of the soul—and intellectually. Moreover, Scripture in some way re-establishes that harmony between body and soul which was disrupted by original sin. Sacred Scripture is like a soothing balm which penetrates our lives and continually heals—insofar as is possible on this earth—the division brought about by sin.

The sacred writer continues, saying that Scripture "judges the reflections and thoughts of the heart." Often, when we meditate on the Scriptures, placing our soul in the presence of God, we find ourselves changed at the end, or perhaps troubled, because we have felt ourselves judged, since the word of God penetrates us and changes our whole way of thinking: judging us, criticizing us, transforming us. The word of God possesses the attributes of God: it continually renews us in every way.

Scripture also produces other spiritual effects as we see from the words of Paul: "And now I commend you to God and to the word of his grace, which is able to build you up and to give you the inheritance among all those who are sanctified [that is, heaven]" (Acts 20:32 RSV). Paul is leaving Miletus and, speaking to the elders who have come from Ephesus, he says that now that he is leaving, he is entrusting them to God and to his word (Sacred Scripture) "which is able to build you up." The word of God is "edifying" not only in the sense that it stimulates us to goodness, but also in the sense that it builds up the life of God in our soul until it brings us to our inheritance in heaven. Besides being alive and active, penetrating and judging, the word of God causes us to advance in the spiritual life. It builds up the Christian life in us, and in so doing it builds up Christ. In building up Christ it brings us to our eternal inheritance.

Paul leaves in peace because he knows who will take care of his flock when he has gone. Even in the event that he has not given the communities' leaders adequate formation, they have the word of God, which he regards as a teacher who will lead them all on to salvation.

In conclusion, let me quote Paul's letter to the Romans: "I am not ashamed of the gospel. It is the power of God leading everyone who believes in it to salvation " (Rom. 1:16). For Paul this power is the power of the God incarnate. It is awesome: it gives charisms, transforms, works miracles, saves. It is the power of God for the salvation of all believers.

4

THE NEW COMMANDMENT

In reading the Gospels, I never fail to be struck by the beauty of Jesus' teaching on love of neighbor, as I see it unfold before me. The subject first appears in Matthew when a group of Pharisees tries to entrap Jesus.

> When the Pharisees heard that he had silenced the Sadducees, they assembled in a body; and one of them, a lawyer, in an attempt to trip him up, asked him, "Teacher, which commandment of the law is the greatest?" Jesus said to him:
> "'You shall Love the Lord your God
> with your whole heart,
> with your whole soul,
> and with all your mind.'
> This is the greatest and first commandment. The second is like it:
> 'You shall love your neighbor as yourself.'
> On these two commandments the whole law is based, and the prophets as well." (Mt. 22:34-40).

Even though this passage contains quotations

from the Old Testament, it clearly belongs to the revelation of Jesus, for if we compare the Old Testament teaching on love of neighbor with what we find stated here, the differences stand out clearly.

The Old Testament commandment to love God is found in Deuteronomy:

> Hear, O Israel! The Lord is our God, the Lord alone! Therefore, you shall love the Lord, your God, with all your heart, and with all your soul, and with all your strength. Take to heart these words which I enjoin on you today. Drill them into your children. Speak of them at home and abroad, whether you are busy or at rest. Bind them at your wrist as a sign and let them be as a pendant on your forehead. Write them on the doorposts of your houses and on your gates (Dt. 6:4-9 NAB).

As you see, the commandment to love God, which we find in the Gospel, is clearly a reiteration of this revelation given in the Pentateuch, when God wants to teach the people of Israel that there is only one God, the Creator of all things, and wants to safeguard them from the temptations of superstition and idolatry.

What we encounter in this passage is a God who is above all things, a God who is so great that his name cannot even be uttered, a God who must therefore be adored and loved with all one's heart and with all one's soul. This is the most majestic passage in the Old Testament. It reveals the existence of God, of the One who is and who is everything for the people of Israel—their only refuge and their only strength—and who therefore has a right to their greatest love.

But love of neighbor is not mentioned here. We find it, instead, in the book of Leviticus, in the midst of a series of admonitions God is giving to his people so that they will live as good Israelites:

> "You shall not go about spreading slander among your kinsmen; nor shall you stand by idly when your neighbor's life is at stake. Take no revenge and cherish no grudge against your fellow countrymen. You shall love your neighbor as yourself. I am the Lord" (Lev. 19:16,18 NAB).

This command is not given a position of importance comparable to that given the command to love God. Moreover, it is not phrased, "Love everyone as yourself," but, "Love your neighbor as yourself." And "neighbor" in this context means another member of the people of Israel.

By contrast, in the Gospel, when Jesus is asked, "Which commandment of the Law is the greatest?" he does not reply with a single commandment, but with two, linking the commandment to love God (which the Jews undoubtedly already recognized as the greatest) with the commandment to love one's neighbor: "You shall love the Lord your God with your whole heart, with your whole soul, and with all your mind. This is the greatest and first commandment. The second is like it. . . ." This is the revelation of Jesus: that there is another commandment, which though not directly concerned with God, is similar to the commandment to love God: "Love your neighbor as yourself."

One would not be far wrong in claiming that this revelation is foreshadowed and implicitly present in the Old Testament, and that what Jesus has done is to spell it out more clearly, since he did not come to destroy the Law but to fulfill it.

In another Gospel passage, however, our Lord further clarifies what love of neighbor means. The explanation is occasioned by the question of an expert on the Law who asks, "And who is my neighbor?" (Lk. 10:29) since, as we have noted, in the Old Testament "neighbor" meant another Israelite.

We must keep in mind at this point that, as Christians, we are used to giving a Christian interpretation to the word "neighbor." For us a "neighbor" is anyone who happens to be near us, anyone we meet on the street—whoever he or she may be. But in Jesus' day, this was not so. And that is why Jesus responds to this question with a parable.

> "There was a man going down from Jerusalem to Jericho who fell prey to robbers. They stripped him, beat him, and then went off leaving him half-dead. A priest happened to be going down the same road; he saw him but continued on. Likewise there was a Levite who came the same way; he saw him and went on. But a Samaritan who was journeying along came on him and was moved to pity at the sight. He approached him and dressed his wounds, pouring in

oil and wine. He then hoisted him on his own beast and brought him to an inn, where he cared for him. The next day he took out two silver pieces and gave them to the innkeeper with the request: 'Look after him, and if there is any further expense I will repay you on my way back.'

"Which of these three, in your opinion, was neighbor to the man who fell in with the robbers?" The answer came, "The one who treated him with compassion." Jesus said to him, "Then go and do the same" (Lk. 10:30-37).

"Who is my neighbor?" Based on the aforementioned passage in Leviticus, possible answers might be: "a blood relative," "a fellow clansman," or "a fellow Israelite."

But Jesus' reply is clear: "Which of these three, in your opinion, was neighbor to the man who fell in with the robbers?" That is, "Which man behaved as a blood relative toward the man who had fallen among robbers?"

The word "neighbor" is still used here in its traditional meaning of "kinsman," but the new type of kinship Jesus presents to us is one based not on blood ties or on membership in the same religious group, but rather on a new religious lifestyle, a spiritually motivated mode of behavior. From now on, therefore, "Love your neighbor" means "Look upon every person you meet as someone who is related to you."

In order to ensure that his listeners understand just what he means by "neighbor," Jesus illustrates his point with an extreme example: a Samaritan. The Samaritans had come from the region of Babylon and had settled among the people of Israel. To a certain extent they had adopted the Jewish religion, but they were not Jewish by race, by tradition, or even by religion, since they had not accepted Judaism entirely. They had built a temple on Mount Gerizim in which they worshipped God without the use of images. However, they did not recognize the temple in Jerusalem and, in addition, they had set up their own priesthood in opposition to the priesthood in Jerusalem.

Their physical proximity to the Jews, combined with the similarity of the two religions and the spirit of opposition, made for constant hatred between Jews and Samaritans. This is reflected in the Gospel espisode of Jesus and the Samaritan woman at the well. When he speaks to her, she is surprised and replies: "What? You are a Jew and you ask me, a Samaritan, for a drink?" John comments, "Jews, in fact, do not associate with Samaritans" (Jn. 4:9 JER).

The word "neighbor," which in the context of the Old Testament might seem applicable only to members of a particular ethnic or religious group, is now revealed in its true meaning: we must go beyond all human barriers and love all people, even our enemies.

Another wonderful passage in Jesus' progressive revelation regarding love of neighbor is to be found

THE NEW COMMANDMENT 51

in Matthew's Gospel when Jesus speaks of the Last Judgment:

> Then the King will say to those on his right hand, "Come, you whom my Father has blessed, take for your heritage the kingdom prepared for you since the foundation of the world. For I was hungry and you gave me food; I was thirsty and you gave me drink; I was a stranger and you made me welcome; naked and you clothed me, sick and you visited me, in prison and you came to see me." Then the virtuous will say to him in reply, "Lord, when did we see you hungry and feed you; or thirsty and give you drink? When did we see you a stranger and make you welcome; naked and clothe you; sick or in prison and go to see you?" And the King will answer, "I tell you solemnly, in so far as you did this to one of the least of these brothers of mine, you did it to me" (Mt. 25:34-40 JER).

The love Jesus speaks of in this passage is more than a mere love of "neighbor"—even when love of neighbor extends beyond family relationships and transcends the barriers of race, religion, and language. Here he explicity indicates that we are to love all who are sick or suffering, and even those who are in prison. (Note that he does not say that we should first look to see whether they are guilty or innocent.) He wants our love to encompass all the situations in human life.

Furthermore, Jesus reveals that when we love our neighbor we are loving *him*.

Now we begin to see why Jesus linked the two commandments in his answer to the lawyer. Christ is present in some way in every human being. When the Word became flesh, he took on a supernatural solidarity with the whole human race. And this is why in loving our neighbor we love God. Our fellow human beings thus become a sacrament, a visible sign of God's presence in the world.

Let us set aside, for now, the many other things which could be said, and move on to the key passage in Jesus' revelation about loving our neighbor. We find it in John's Gospel in the account of the Last Supper when Jesus utters the most beautiful and most sublime words in all of Revelation: "This is my commandment: love one another as I have loved you" (John 15:12).

Here, other persons are no longer considered only as objects of our love, but as subjects capable of loving. The first new element we notice in this expression is that Jesus not only states that love of neighbor is the greatest commandment—as he had already declared to the lawyer—but he says that it is *his* commandment.

In the rabbinical schools of the time it was common practice to pose the question: "What is the most important precept of the Law?" Every doctor of the Law, every teacher in Israel, gave his own answer, his particular theological, ascetical, spiritual, and moral synthesis. From these characteristic norms one could distinguish the disciples of the various teachers. Each of these schools was rich in content and tradition. The archeological discoveries at Qumran near the Dead Sea have disclosed a

THE NEW COMMANDMENT

gold mine of information about one such theological and spiritual school of the time.

It was quite important, therefore, for Jesus' disciples to know which was the key point of their spiritual and moral life, to know what was the point of encounter between revealed doctrine and practical living. They needed to know what way of life would make it clear to others that Jesus' disciples were followers of a revelation from heaven, followers of the one and triune God whom Christ had made known to them.

At the Last Supper Jesus makes all this clear to us by giving us his commandment and adding, "By this love you have for one another, everyone will know that you are my disciples" (Jn. 13:35 JER). This sentence sheds still more light on what Jesus means by love of neighbor. He wants us to love *as he loves*. It is not enough to be merely polite or pleasantly agreeable, or to show signs of affection. Even a compassionate concern for others which leads to the giving of material goods is not sufficient. Human love in all its fullness and with all its nuances is not enough. We must love as Jesus loves, with a heart both human and divine.

That is why this is *his* commandment: because in order to carry it out we must become children of God, we must be taken into the life of the Trinity.

Jesus' commandment also contains the idea of reciprocity. Our love for our neighbor will not be full and perfect if it does not become reciprocal with other disciples of Jesus.

Seen in this perspective, human nature appears

in a completely new light. It becomes much clearer that a bond exists between myself and my neighbor, that I need my neighbor. Alone I can never carry out this typically Christian commandment. Only in the context of a community can I carry it out fully and completely.

Jesus' revelation not only provides a deeper understanding of human nature, it also shows that human love can be raised up to participate in that communion of love which, from all eternity, the Father, Son, and Holy Spirit have shared in heaven. Here on earth, this loving communion among the persons of the Trinity is most clearly and visibly manifested in the human-divine love of Jesus' disciples. This love makes of them a human-divine community: the Church.

"By this," Jesus said, "everyone will know that you are my disciples." For this sort of love cannot exist without a special outpouring of the Holy Spirit, without Jesus being spiritually present in the midst of his disciples who thereby become witnesses to his doctrine and to his charismatic presence in the world.

5

JESUS IN OUR MIDST

The presence of Jesus in the community is a fundamental aspect of our spirituality and one of those points most characteristic of our Movement. Nonetheless, it is a difficult topic to deal with.

Prior to Vatican II, Jesus' words, "Where two or three are gathered in my name, there am I in their midst" (Mt. 18:20), were very rarely mentioned. Throughout the entire history of the Church, except for the Council of Chalcedon[18] (451), the sentence was almost never cited in the more solemn documents of the councils. By contrast, there is not a single document of Vatican II which does not mention this fundamental concept. We find it in the *Decree on the Apostolate of the Laity*,[19] which states that the reason why it is good for the laity to carry out apostolic activities together is to be found in Jesus' promise: "Where two or three are gathered in my name, there am I in their midst." We find it as well in the *Constitution on the Sacred Liturgy*[20] and in the *Decree on the Renewal of the Religious*

Life.[21] But this idea, which is undoubtedly the soul of the Council, is most evident in the Council's statement on collegiality.[22]

It is both a sign of the times, and a sign that the Movement is the work of the Holy Spirit, that the Movement is so in tune with the directives of the Ecumenical Council.

But let us examine the meaning of this doctrine more closely, by considering how it is presented to us in various places throughout the Gospels. Our first passage is from the Sermon on the Mount.

> If you bring your gift to the altar and there recall that your brother has anything against you, leave your gift at the altar, go first to be reconciled with your brother, and then come and offer your gift (Mt. 5:23-24).

Here Jesus is trying to bring out the fact that his revelation is new, the true fulfillment of all that had been revealed up to that time. Before speaking these words he had said:

> You have heard the commandment imposed on your forefathers, "You shall not commit murder; every murderer shall be liable to judgment." What I say to you is: everyone who grows angry with his brother shall be liable to judgment; any man who uses abusive language toward his brother shall be answerable to the Sanhedrin, and if he holds him in contempt he risks the fires of Gehenna (Mt. 5:21-22).

After this, we would have expected him to continue: "So if you have offended your brother, before going to the altar to offer your gift, go and make peace with your brother." Instead he says, "If you recall that your brother has anything against you, leave your gift at the altar, go first to be reconciled with your brother." Jesus does not tell us the obvious: "If you have offended your brother, make peace." Rather, he tells us, "If your brother has something against you, make peace with him."

Scripture scholars have tried to understand whether or not Jesus was speaking only of those cases where the "brother" in question would have a just reason for having something against us. The most respected exegetes have concluded that Jesus was undoubtedly referring to trivial matter, and not to just causes; otherwise he would have said: "If you have done something to your brother and he, therefore, rightly has something against you, go and make peace." But Jesus simply says, "If your brother has something against you. . . ."

Jesus wants us to realize that our rapport with our neighbor is an important part of our relationship with God; it is not an unrelated matter. Before we can go to God, we must first have established a loving relationship among ourselves, having overcome not only those divisions which occur when I wrong my neighbor, but also those which occur when he or she wrongs me for a petty or unjustified reason. When I appear before God, I must already be united with my neighbor.

58 REACHING FOR MORE

This view completely changes the pre-Christian concept of things. However, we Christians still often think of our relationship with God in purely personal terms, considering our neighbor merely as a means to get to God. In other words, our rapport with God is mostly "God-I," whereas in this Scripture passage it is quite clear that there must also be a "God-we" dimension to this rapport. I cannot go to God if I am not in accord with my neighbors.

> You have heard the commandment imposed on your forefathers, "Do not take a false oath; rather, make good to the Lord all your pledges." What I tell you is: do not swear at all. Do not swear by heaven (it is God's throne), nor by the earth (it is his footstool), nor by Jerusalem (it is the city of the great King); do not swear by your head (you cannot make a single hair white or black). Say, "Yes" when you mean "Yes" and "No" when you mean "No." Anything beyond that is from the evil one (Mt. 5:33-37).

At first, these words, too, appear somewhat mysterious. Jesus forbids the taking of oaths—and not merely false oaths. Yet we know that in the course of the Church's history oaths have been taken, beginning with Paul himself: "I call on God as my witness that it was out of consideration for you that I did not come to Corinth again" (2 Cor. 1:23). Scholars have pondered over the meaning of the phrase, "Do not swear at all," on the basis of which some Christian denominations forbid all oaths. The exegetes have concluded that Jesus intended these words not as an instruction for individual behavior, but rather as an indication that the life of the Christian community should be such that oaths become superfluous. He wanted Christians to live with one another in such truth that it would be enough to say "Yes" or "No." In fact the need to support a statement with an oath stems from mistrust on the part of the hearer or previous untruthfulness on the part of the speaker. That is why Jesus says: "Anything beyond that is from the evil one," because it comes from distrust or a lack of truthfulness.

Even this brief passage, therefore, indicates how strongly Jesus desires that Christianity be lived in such a profound communitarian way that those external forms which people resort to as a remedy for disunity will be rendered unnecessary. Remedies may certainly be used, but they will be a sign that Christians are not fully living their Christianity *together*.

Evidently, even in Paul's time there was not that profound unity which Jesus desired.

Let us move on to consider a sentence from the "Our Father": "And forgive us the wrong we have done as we forgive those who wrong us" (Mt. 6:12). This is also a difficult sentence to understand, for we would be inclined to pray: "I am bad, and I certainly don't forgive all the things I should; but at least you, God, forgive me." Instead Jesus teaches us to pray "And forgive us the wrong we have done as we forgive those who wrong us." This prayer would be incomprehensible were it not for the fact that a real bond exists between me and my neighbors. For if my rapport with God were completely independent from my rapport with others, it would be better for God to pardon me all my offenses so that then I would find it easier to pardon others. Instead, Jesus wants us to ask to be forgiven in the measure that we forgive, because this way is more just, more constructive, more useful. Actually, if we look at what we ask in the "Our Father," we see that Jesus wants us to ask for more than mere forgiveness. We actually ask that we might be instruments of forgiveness for our neighbor, and that the measure of our love toward others be equal to God's love toward us.

This means that there is a strong, deep bond between myself and my neighbor. It indicates that we must go toward God together.

Our prayer must be an expression of our communion with others, and only in this way will it be true prayer. And only then will God accept and answer it.

In short, Jesus leads us to an ever-fuller awareness that we are, and must consider ourselves to be, bound to one another.

In Matthew's Gospel we find yet another passage with a similar message: "Do not judge, and you will not be judged; because the judgments you give are the judgments you will get, and the amount you measure out is the amount you will be given" (Mt. 7:1-2 JER). Jesus is urging us not to judge, but he is also telling us in all seriousness that God will deal with us just as we have dealt with our neighbor.

Here my relationship with my neighbor is almost identified with my relationship with God; God acts towards me as I act toward my neighbor. Here again we glimpse that God is identifying himself in some way with our neighbor. Moreover, as in the "Our Father," my neighbor and myself are put on the same level.

Further on, we find another passage which clearly brings us closer to the mystery of Christ's presence among us: "Again I tell you, if two of you join your voices on earth to pray for anything whatever, it shall be granted you by my Father in heaven" (Mt. 18:19). Up to this point we have looked at statements which approach the matter from what we might call a negative point of view. In other words, the bond between me and my neighbor is highlighted by speaking of the faults I must avoid (Do not judge, etc.). Here, instead, Jesus shows the positive side of this bond with my neighbor: "Again I tell you, if two of you join your voices on earth to pray for anything whatever, it shall be granted you by my Father in heaven."

This is a well-known passage; but what needs to be pointed out is the explanation which follows it: The reason we will be granted anything we ask is that "where two or three are gathered in my name, there am I in their midst" (Mt. 18:20).

First of all we should note that although the Gospel indicates that we will obtain what we ask for if we are united in Jesus' name, it does not say that Jesus is present in our midst *only* when we are praying. Evidently, however, he is present *also* when we are united in prayer, and that is why we receive what we ask for. But we will return to this passage further on.

In the process of revealing to us the Gospel message concerning the communitarian aspects of our Christian life, Jesus said one thing which sums up his entire teaching: "This is my commandment: love one another as I have loved you. . . . The command I give you is this, that you love one another" (Jn. 15:12,17).

Previous to this, in teaching about love, he had told us to love God and to love our neighbor. But now that the time has come for him to give us his commandment regarding love, Jesus no longer tells us to love God or to love our neighbor; he no longer merely commands us to see him in our neighbor or to treat every stranger as our neighbor. When it comes to specifying what *his* love is, and how he wants Christian love to be, he says, "This is my commandment: love one another." Jesus wants the Church to be a community of persons who love. An individual, personal love for God or for our neighbor is not enough, because love for neighbor is not full and complete until it becomes reciprocal.

Jesus did not say simply: "Each of you should love the others," but rather: "Love one another as I have loved you." He wants reciprocal love to be at the basis of our Christian life. This is all part of the mystery that we must go to God together. We cannot go to God alone; and if our love is not reciprocal, it is not that perfect, Christian love which Jesus demands of us.

Nonetheless, we are very much accustomed to thinking in terms of our own personal journey to God and to seeing others as mere instruments for our sanctification. Therefore, we must rid ourselves of this outmoded way of thinking.

As regards the commands we are to put into practice, this represents the high point of all Jesus' revelation. It is the synthesis of all that is contained in his previous teachings and commands. And therefore he says, "This is my commandment."

However, all this would still remain somewhat mysterious, were it not for the fact that revelation has shed additional light on its meaning. In John's Gospel, we find that after giving us his basic commandment, Jesus continues:

> I am the true vine, and my Father is the vinedresser. Every branch in me that bears no fruit he cuts away, and every branch that does bear fruit he prunes to make it bear even more. You are pruned already, by means of the word that I have spoken to you. Make your home in me, as I make mine in you. As a branch cannot bear fruit all by itself, but must remain part of the vine, neither can you unless you remain in me. I am the vine, you are the branches. Whoever remains in me, with me in him, bears fruit in plenty; for cut off

from me you can do nothing. Anyone who does not remain in me is like a branch that has been thrown away—he withers (Jn. 15:1-6 JER).

Having given us his commandment, Jesus goes on to explain the more mysterious depths of his revelation, using the now-familiar image of himself as a plant—the grapevine—and we Christians as the branches who are nourished by the divine life which circulates throughout this plant.

This image reveals to us that we are partakers of the divine life which is in Jesus, and that this divine "sap" unites us to one another as branches that are united to the trunk.

Now we can begin to understand the reason behind all Jesus' previous teachings. We have already seen that we must go to God together and not alone, that we must deal with our neighbor in a special way, and that alone we cannot live the greatest commandment in all its fullness. Now Jesus begins to explain why this is so, telling us that all together we are like a single plant, and that in all of us there is one life which we share with one another and with him.

This revelation is already very enlightening, but Jesus wished to give us even greater light through the teaching of Paul, who explains the Christian life as the life of a body, the very body of Christ. Christ is its head, and all Christians are its members: "We, though many, are one body in Christ" (Rom. 12:5). "You, then, are the body of Christ. Every one of you is a member of it" (1 Cor. 12:27).

Thus we understand why we must be reconciled with our "brother" when we bring our gift to the altar. We are both part of the one body of Christ. True, I am an individual; and in going toward God I still retain my personality and individuality. But my neighbor and I are already so bound to one another by the divine lymph of the supernatural life, by the life of God, that we are a single reality.

Therefore I must make peace, not only with those whom I have offended, but also with those whom I have not offended, because they are part of me. Otherwise I am going to God without a part of myself.

Moreover, if we are one body, this body must be truthful and sincere with itself. And this will not be so, if it finds it necessary to use language which is not simply "yes" to mean "yes" and "no" to mean "no." Jesus does not say that it is wrong to take oaths, but rather that the need to do so comes from the evil one. We must be able to do without them.

"Forgive us the wrong we have done as we forgive those who wrong us." "Do not judge." These words reflect still other characteristics of the life we are meant to live.

Even before revealing that we are all part of the one vine, that there is one divine life which is in all of us, and that we are one body, the body of Christ, Jesus had told us all this with the words: "Where two or three are gathered in my name, there am I in their midst." This was an anticipation of what he was still to reveal in the course of his preaching.

Both Paul's explanation of the Mystical Body

and the Gospel image of the vine and the branches are rather general and, therefore, still somewhat removed from our personal experience. But the words, "Where two or three are gathered in my name, there am I in their midst" give us a complete and precise application of the whole of Christian doctrine, and clarify for us what it means to be one body: where two persons are united in his name, there is Jesus.

When we are united in his name, Jesus is present. It is he who unites us; without his presence we could not be united. Therefore, *ipso facto*, if we are united it means that Jesus is in our midst.

What depth there is to these words! They contain the whole mystery of the Church, the whole mystery of the Mystical Body. Yet they can be lived now, in this very moment, because the mystery of the Church is one that concerns each of us in every moment—not only on the day of our baptism or when we go to church, but always, every day.

All things considered, it seems to me that Christians today—and that includes us—are in need of a conversion. In the past we frequently conceived of the Christian life as consisting entirely in the personal rapport between ourselves and God. This rapport is certainly important, but we must now make a new discovery: that the entire Christian life is also contained in the rapport between my neighbor and myself. In this rapport I find God and I am able to draw closer to him.

Our Movement is one of the expressions of the Church's current rediscovery of the communitarian

Christian life. When each of us met the Movement, we felt many of our longings fulfilled. These longings, however, were actually the longings of our world today, since all of us are immersed in the world and to a greater or lesser degree we have all shared in humanity's current struggles.

The young man or woman who is not concerned with the problems of humanity as such, but is concerned instead with his or her own family, future, sufferings, worries or difficulties, often does not realize that these very sufferings are a result of all the trouble and pain in the world around us. The particular problems he or she experiences are nothing other than a reflection, an echo of all the disorder and suffering which surround us and in which each of us is immersed.

The great problems of humanity do not leave us unaffected; on the contrary, they touch us intimately—frequently through problems that to us seem personal and limited. Each of us has experienced this sort of suffering. Many others, however, are acutely aware of the problems that afflict society and humanity, because they experience them firsthand.

Besides the problem presented by the social dimension of human nature, that is, the problem of the relationship of each person with society, with humanity, there is another grave challenge facing humanity today: that of the relationship of each person with himself or herself.

This struggle is evident in the various individualistic, existentialist philosophies of our day. In philosophy, theology, literature and other areas of thought, it is expressed in a search for self, for the answers to the questions: "What am I?" "Who am I?" "Why do I exist?" It is a cause of great torment to many people.

Although we may not always experience this torment on an intellectual level, nonetheless it affects us and causes us to suffer, to feel a certain lack of unity within ourselves: we are not what we would like to be; we are unsuccessful in being what we ought to be. All of us have experienced the painful awareness of this inner wound.

When we discover the communitarian dimension of Christianity, and especially when we meet a community which incarnates this dimension, we find the solution to all our personal and social problems.

Many of you can identify with this experience, because when you met the Movement you found not only the answer to your own personal problems but, in a nutshell, the answer to the problems of many others. In fact, all problems can be resolved with this same solution: that is, with the presence of God as found in the Christian community and with the presence of Christ's truth in society.

This is what today's world is waiting for: the discovery that the solution to the problem of who we are and of how to experience inner unity is found in being united with God, in giving ourselves to him, and in finding ourselves in him. In this rapport with God, the problem of our relationship with others is also resolved, since, as we have seen, God identifies himself with our neighbor.

As Christians in today's world, we are called to share this discovery with everyone.

6

JESUS FORSAKEN

About midafternoon, Jesus on the cross cried out in a loud voice, "My God, my God, why have you forsaken me?" (Mt. 27:46; Mk. 15:34). What mysterious words! Even those present did not understand what he was saying.

His words are recorded for us by two evangelists, in Hebrew and Aramaic respectively. Matthew writes, "Eli, Eli, lema sabachthani?" and Mark, "Eloi, Eloi, lama sabachthani?" Scripture scholars have speculated about the language in which Jesus actually said these words, and they generally agree that he uttered them in Aramaic, the dialect spoken at that time. These same words are the opening words of Psalm 22, a messianic psalm describing the physical and emotional suffering that the Messiah was to undergo during his crucifixion.

However, it was not because he intended to recite this psalm to show that he was the Messiah that Jesus cried out these words from the cross. No. During the crucifixion he actually felt the same sufferings that had been foretold in the psalm.

The text of the psalm speaks of a just man surrounded by powerful enemies, who feels that God is abandoning him. His cry is not one of despair, but an invocation to God. In fact the psalm concludes with a hymn of trust in God, who would certainly free the just man from his enemies and make him victorious.

From this simple analysis, we can already see that Jesus' cry, "My God, my God, why have you forsaken me?"—which reflects the same sentiments as the psalm—is indeed an expression of extreme suffering, but also of absolute confidence in what God would do.

Moreover, it is beautiful to see that Jesus chose to repeat these words not in Hebrew, the language in which most of Scripture was written, but in Aramaic, the language spoken by the people. In other words, he was going through the same spiritual suffering described in the psalm, but he expressed it in the language he used every day.

Since it is our point of reference, let us look at Psalm 22 and examine the meaning of the word "forsaken." We find that the Hebrew does not indicate a desire on God's part to abandon Jesus, but rather its precise significance is "to leave someone in a painful situation without intervening." The psalm depicts a person who is surrounded by lions and other ferocious beasts, but no one intervenes to free him. This being the case, a better translation might be "Why are you leaving me in this condition?" rather than "Why have you forsaken me?"

Both Gospels have expressed this in their

inspired translation by rendering the Hebrew and Aramaic verbs with the Greek *enkataleipo* (*leipo* means "to leave behind"; *en* indicates a state or condition; *kata* here indicates a negative situation—as in the English "cataclysm," "catastrophe," etc.).

Therefore, from a linguistic point of view we can determine that when Jesus said these words he felt abandoned by the Father in the sense that the Father had not intervened on his behalf and had left him in this terrible, painful situation. His suffering is an indication of his deep personal rapport with the Father.

But if Jesus was truly God and man, how could he have suffered any separation from the Father or felt abandoned by him in any way? At this point we are face to face with the greatest mystery of our religion: the Incarnation.

Generally we are not sufficiently aware of who Jesus truly is. We know that he is God and that he is man, a human being like each of us. But we must keep in mind that this human being is substantially and hypostatically united to God, and that therefore, as a human being, he possesses gifts and graces which we will never have.

This is such a great mystery that we will never be able to comprehend it fully, because it is part of the very mystery of God and of how God could become incarnate and take on human nature.

Let us now consider the various types of knowledge which Jesus possessed. We human beings are born as *tabulae rasae* (blank slates), according to an old philosophical expression, and we use information we receive through our senses to formulate concepts. But according to theologians, throughout his life on earth Jesus possessed the Beatific Vision. This means that he saw God face to face, whereas we will see God in this way only in the next life, in heaven. As you know, the Beatific Vision is a completely spiritual type of knowledge; it is not derived from sense experience. In fact it is impossible to reach the point of being able to see God with our senses. The Beatific Vision is independent of our senses and of our bodily development; Jesus possessed it from the first moment of his conception. While still in Mary's womb he saw God, the Blessed Trinity, because, since his soul was spiritually complete from the very first moment, he was able to possess and enjoy the Beatific Vision fully.

According to theologians, Jesus also had a second type of knowledge which only a few saints have possessed (and these only partially): infused knowledge; that is, he knew created things as they really are. He knew the most holy things as well as the things of this world, and he knew them from the time he was an infant, because of this knowledge which was directly infused into his soul by God.

Jesus' divinity penetrated every part of his human nature and, therefore, as a human being he possessed every possible perfection.

In addition to all this, Jesus had the type of knowledge that we have: the knowledge derived from experience. However, this ordinary human knowledge was not perfect in him from the beginning, because—unlike infused knowledge and the Beatific Vision—it is related to bodily growth and development. Therefore it increased with age. In Jesus, these three ways of knowing were distinct realities and were not in conflict with one another.

For example, Jesus knew that he would die, and that he would also suffer the abandonment of the Father; yet when he actually experienced it, he acquired a new knowledge of it. From the point of view of his human experience, it was a totally new and painful reality.

Some ancient Church writers, and apparently even Saint Ambrose,[23] interpreted Jesus' cry of abandonment as an expression of separation from the Godhead. This hypothesis, however, was immediately and universally rejected by theologians because if Jesus' human nature had been separated from the Divinity in the moment of the Passion and Redemption, then the Redemption would not have been the work of the God-man, and would therefore not have an infinite value. So not only was Jesus' divinity united to his humanity in that moment, but as a human being he also possessed all of the consequences of this union: namely, the Beatific Vision and infused knowledge.

What was utterly new in that moment was that Jesus as a human being experienced in himself separation from God and the Father's non-intervention.

In that moment he felt himself covered by our sins. But how could Jesus have felt himself covered with sin, when he was absolutely sinless? As a

JESUS FORSAKEN

human being, not only had he not sinned, but he was incapable of sinning, since his human nature was hypostatically united to the divine nature. The answer is that Jesus was united to the whole human race. Though as an individual he was united to the Divinity, through his physical body he was united to the whole of humanity. Physically, he was a descendant of Adam and Eve, Abraham, and the Patriarchs.

Jesus was free from original sin, conceived as he was in the womb of the immaculate Virgin Mary. But he willed to experience in his own human nature the consequences of sin and the pain of the separation brought about by sin. He had not the least trace of sin, nor had he ever sinned, but he willed to take upon himself the same human condition as the rest of the human race which was still weighed down by the consequence of original sin.

For example, let us imagine a family in which one member has committed a crime such as murder. The other members of the family are innocent, yet when they meet people on the street they feel the weight of this crime on their shoulders because they are blood relatives.

In Jesus' case there was the bond of blood relationship and much more, because he had mystically united himself to the whole human race.

Because he had taken on our human flesh, and in that flesh all humanity was contained, he experienced the pain of separation from the Father, and so brought about the Redemption. In fact, by surrendering himself to the Father, by offering his suffering to him, he merited not only the glorification of his own body but also the redemption of the whole human race—the redemption of each of us.

The mystery of Jesus forsaken is linked to many other mysteries. One of these is the manner in which he as an individual is united to the whole human race. He is so fully one with humanity that he takes upon himself the consequences of sin, bears the pain of these consequences, and, with an act of love, reunites each of us and the whole of humanity with God.

Another mystery is that, although Jesus always possessed the Beatific Vision, his body was not glorified until after the Resurrection. Only after the Redemption was accomplished did his body become impassible, glorious, and full of light as our glorified bodies will be in heaven after our resurrection. This reveals yet again how intimately bound we are to Jesus, and he to us. Paul tells us that on the cross Jesus merited the glorification of his body and acquired the right for his name to be glorified:

> . . . he humbled himself,
>   obediently accepting even death,
>   death on a cross!
> Because of this,
>   God highly exalted him
>   and bestowed on him the name
>   above every other name,
> So that at Jesus' name
>   every knee must bend
>   in the heavens, on the earth,
>   and under the earth (Phil. 2:8-11).

Thomas Aquinas posed the question: "Was the Redemption accomplished during the course of Jesus' passion or at the moment of his death?"[24] He replies that the Redemption came about through the whole painful process that began with the agony in the garden and climaxed in Jesus' death. With his death and resurrection the Redemption was brought to conclusion.

Even though the Redemption came about as a result of all Jesus' spiritual and physical sufferings, the greatest suffering, the one which symbolizes the whole Redemption, occurred in the moment in which he felt separated from the Father. It was then that he brought about the reunification of humanity with the Father. Jesus forsaken is the symbol, the sign, the definite indication of the Redemption. We see in his experience of abandonment the perfect example of the suffering through which the human race was redeemed; for the Redemption was accomplished through the suffering of the abandonment, which permeated all Jesus' other sufferings and gave them meaning. Even the physical agony he went through was intensified by the pain of separation from the Father, expressed in his cry, "My God, my God, why have you forsaken me?"

Some have asked the question, "When did Jesus suffer most during his passion?" The answer is: when he cried out, "My God, my God, why have you forsaken me?" This is because spiritual sufferings are much more painful than physical sufferings, and the greatest spiritual suffering is the experience of separation from God caused by sin.

Sin is the most terrible thing in the world; it is an affront against God. Therefore when Jesus experienced in his soul the sufferings of humanity, which had sinned against God and had separated itself from him, he experienced the greatest pain he could ever have experienced. In that moment he experienced a suffering which no other human being can ever experience, because, though human, he was personally united to the Divinity; he was the God-man.

This suffering is of infinite value for all of us because the one who experienced it was God, God who in his human nature underwent the pain of the separation caused by sin. And he experienced it not as something outside himself but as something personal, since he had willed to take on human nature and to become a member of the very human race which had sinned against him.

All of us were spiritually present in Jesus, united to his human nature because of God's design that he should sum up all humanity in himself. Each of us individually was also present in his soul, because with the Beatific Vision and his infused knowledge Jesus knew all those who had ever lived, who were living at that moment, and who would ever live. His perfectly intelligent soul was aware not only of all the persons who would ever exist, but also of all the movements that would ever arise in the Church—including, certainly, that Movement which would make his cry "My God, my God, why have you forsaken me?" the mainstay of its spirituality.

In the moment in which he accepted all his sufferings he also took upon himself all our misdeeds, thereby atoning for them, and said, "Father, into your hands I commend my spirit" (Lk. 23:46).

However, his soul never experienced a moment of hesitation; that is, there was not first a time in which he did not accept his suffering, followed by the moment in which he did accept it. No. When he cried out, "My God, my God, why have you forsaken me?" that cry was already an act of painful acceptance.

When Jesus said, "Father, into your hands I commend my spirit," he wanted to show us that everything had been accomplished, that our sins had been atoned for.

Moreover he obtained for all of us, with whom he was so united, the possibility of becoming him. He did not simply win for us the forgiveness of our sins so that we might be saved; he made us members of his Body.

These concepts are mysterious to us because we are so used to seeing ourselves divided, to looking at ourselves with the eyes of the flesh. But the truth is that we are cells of Christ's Body. And we should not regard this Body as something undefined or vague, or as some sort of association or society. We have been truly—though mysteriously—made members of Christ's Body, and the Holy Spirit is our soul, the soul of the Mystical Body. The Holy Spirit unites us more profoundly than the cells of our physical body, because they are held together by a created human soul, whereas we are united by God, and therefore in a much more perfect way, though we still remain distinct and responsible individuals.

It has often been said that the saints and the religious orders they founded are like moments of Jesus' life which are continuing in the life of the Church; and this is true. Since Christians are members of Christ's body, our life is nothing less than the life of Christ himself—not merely in the sense that he has given us the example of how we must live, but because it is his life that lives in us, that acts in us.

Ours is not a human patience, referred to as Christian merely because we are baptized; it is Christ's own patience living in us. In the same way, Christian love is not a benevolent feeling directed toward Christ. It is Christ's own love which penetrates us and causes us to love others with his love because, by participation, he has made our love divine.

In heaven we will see God face-to-face and we will see our life as it really is. "Now we see indistinctly, as in a mirror; then we shall see face-to-face. My knowledge is imperfect now; then I shall know even as I am known" (1 Cor. 13:12).

If we are to live Christ, we must live the experience Christ lived, and he lived in a pre-eminent way the Redemption of the human race.

The Redemption was the most important act of Jesus' life. All the actions of his human life were of infinite value, but they were all in preparation for the moment in which he would accomplish the Redemption.

The author of the Letter to the Hebrews affirms: "On coming into the world, Jesus said: '... I have come to do your will, O God'" (Heb. 10:5,7). The very first moment he entered this world, Jesus said his "yes" to the suffering of the crucifixion, and his whole life was nothing but a preparation for Calvary, which was the guiding light for his every action, his every word, his every prayer.

For us, then, to relive Jesus crucified and forsaken in our own lives means to identify with his innermost feelings. But it means much more than that. It means allowing those acts of love and suffering which our Lord experienced on the cross to live again in us, through grace. Thus, we too, by suffering out of love, participate in the fulfillment of his passion.

7

THE CALL TO FOLLOW JESUS

A vocation is a call from God, his loving gaze directed at us. We ourselves first experience it at that moment in our lives when we become aware of his love and hear his call. But he has been loving us in this way since before we were born. In fact he has brought us into the world for this very reason—in view of our vocation, of the plan we are meant to accomplish on this earth.

Our vocation is something truly wonderful, because it forms an integral part of our natural and supernatural personality. It is the real meaning behind our life, the reason for everything we will do from now on.

I would like to read with you a few passages of Scripture which describe the calling of the first apostles.

Generally we are so accustomed to thinking of Jesus surrounded by his disciples that we never think of the time when he was preaching alone. Yet, before he called the apostles, Jesus was alone.

THE CALL TO FOLLOW JESUS 83

First, he had prepared himself for thirty years, working in Nazareth, living with Mary and Joseph. Then he too, as a human being, experienced a call: to begin his public life. And his first act was to make a profound spiritual preparation. Certainly Jesus had no need of such a preparation, but he wanted it because as a human being he wanted to live as we would have to live. And after his forty days in the desert he willed to be tempted by the devil, who tempted him with the same basic human desires that all of us feel at some time in our own lives. After this preparation, Jesus began to preach.

However, he felt that he should not be alone in his preaching; so he called others to help him. He knew that he would have to give them some formation, that they were spiritually and humanly rough. But he felt the need to have a small group whom he might teach, to whom he might give of himself, and with whom he might also have a rapport of mutual love. And so we have the call of the disciples.

> As he was walking along the Sea of Galilee he watched two brothers, Simon now known as Peter, and his brother Andrew, casting a net into the sea. They were fishermen. He said to them, "Come after me and I will make you fishers of men." They immediately abandoned their nets and became his followers. He walked along farther and caught sight of two other brothers, James, Zebedee's son, and his brother John. They too were in their boat, getting their nets in order with their father, Zebedee. He called them, and immediately they abandoned boat and father to follow him (Mt. 4:18-22).

"They immediately abandoned their nets and became his followers." We have read or heard this passage countless times. But we ought to try to imagine what actually took place in the souls of these people and made them leave everything and follow Jesus.

Certainly, they must have loved their parents. In addition, they already had an established career— and a rather good one, at that. They were fishermen and had their own boat, their own business.

Then one day they saw Jesus passing by. They had certainly already heard people speaking of him as a preacher inspired by God. But they surely did not know that he was the Son of God. When he passed by, looked at them, and called them, they must have felt something deep within their souls. They must have felt what every person who has a vocation feels when he or she hears Jesus' call. We, too, have had this feeling: that is, a sense that our personality is being fulfilled, that our whole life and all our past experiences—even the negative ones— have now acquired meaning because Jesus is calling us. Jesus is giving a reason to our existence.

To feel a vocation means to find God, and in him, the fullness of our own existence. Everything else then begins to appear in a new light. Whereas before, many things occupied our attention and were important in life—such as family, future, health, and so on—suddenly they are no longer so important. We will continue to be concerned about these things as long as it is God's will, but they will

THE CALL TO FOLLOW JESUS   85

no longer be the determining factors in our lives. In fact, the apostles left everything and followed Jesus.

Further on in the Gospels we read that later—on various occasions during Jesus' public life, and again after his death and resurrection—the apostles returned to fishing. But they did so with a changed attitude. Previously, fishing must have been one of the most important things in their lives; now it was merely a means for earning a living. Their reason for living was no longer to be found in their work, but in following Jesus.

In calling them, Jesus revealed all the love that God had had for them from eternity, and would continue to have for all eternity.

Let us now consider the vocation of the rich young man. His negative response helps us to understand even better what Jesus must have said with his loving gaze to Peter, Andrew, James and John.

> Another time a man came up to him and said, "Teacher, what good must I do to possess everlasting life?" He answered, "Why do you question me about what is good? There is One who is good. If you wish to enter into life, keep the commandments." "Which ones?" he asked. Jesus replied, "'You shall not kill'; 'You shall not commit adultery'; 'You shall not steal'; 'You shall not bear false witness'; 'Honor your father and your mother'; and 'Love your neighbor as yourself.'" The young man said to him, "I have kept all these; what do I need to do further?" Jesus told

him, "If you seek perfection, go, sell your possessions, and give to the poor. You will then have treasure in heaven. Afterward come back and follow me." Hearing these words, the young man went away sad, for his possessions were many (Mt. 19:16-22).

Jesus had already been preaching for some time now, and certainly he had many followers, among whom was this young disciple. We can infer this from the rich young man's words, "I have kept all these," even after Jesus had added "Love your neighbor as yourself." Only one of Jesus' disciples could have understood the full meaning of love of neighbor.

The rich young man had therefore already been fascinated by Jesus. He had followed him, had listened to his teachings, and had tried to put them into practice. That is why Mark says that "Jesus looked at him with love" (Mk. 10:21). Jesus had already looked at him, and had already loved him; but now, in a special way, he showed him his love, the love that God had had for him from all eternity. And he invited him to be his own.

With a vocation, Jesus wants to fill the soul with himself. Therefore, the soul must not be attached to anything else; otherwise it cannot let itself be filled. This is the gift Jesus wanted to give. But even though the rich young man was good, he renounced Jesus' love because he was attached to his wealth.

Watching him go off, Jesus said, "I repeat what I said: it is easier for a camel to pass through a needle's eye than for a rich man to enter the kingdom of God" (Mt. 19:24). At this, the disciples asked, "Then who can be saved?" (Mt. 19:25) and as we all know, Jesus replied: "For man it is impossible; but for God all things are possible" (Mt. 19:26).

Scripture scholars have tried to understand the full meaning of this passage, and to analyze this painful moment in which God showed his love for someone, but the person refused to give himself completely to God. They have wondered whether or not the rich young man was saved.

On the one hand we might think that if someone has heard God's call as clearly as this young man, and yet does not accept it because he is attached to this world's goods, he will not be saved. On the other hand, we have Jesus' consoling words telling us that for God all things are possible. For he has an infinite number of ways to save souls.

What is quite clear is that Jesus wants each person's voluntary, personal adherence to his call. That is, we can say "no" and still be saved. A vocation is not obligatory, something we must necessarily go along with in order to be saved. On the contrary, God in his love wants our response to his call to be spontaneous.

In marriage, for example, the willingness and love of one spouse coupled with the merely passive response of the other is not enough. The free wills of both partners must come together in mutual consent. Without these two free wills, without these two utterly free loves which intertwine, which unite with and strengthen one another, and which are sanctified in the sacrament, there is no marriage.

The situation of a vocation is analogous. The vocation is a loving act of God by which he calls us; but if we look at it only from this perspective, we will not yet understand all its depth and beauty. Just as a marriage becomes a true marriage only when not one, but both partners love one another and want the marriage, in the same way a vocation becomes a true vocation in all its fullness only when it is mutual; that is, when not only God chooses the person, but the person, realizing that he or she is loved by God, chooses him.

One who does not respond to this call loses the possibility of acquiring this special rapport with Jesus.

What has always struck me in the story of the rich young man has been not that he risked losing his soul by not corresponding to his vocation, but rather that God loved him and he rejected that love. To reject God's love is the most terrible thing that one can do.

God's call is one of the most beautiful things in the world. Just think of the interaction of love, of the intertwining of divine and human wills that occurs in a vocation! A vocation lasts for all eternity, because God is eternity; it is a profound and continuing love that will live on forever.

We cannot fully realize or understand what an immense grace a vocation is; or rather—to avoid using the worn-out term *vocation*—what a grace it is to feel God's personal love as he calls us to follow him.

THE CALL TO FOLLOW JESUS 89

A person who begins to sense that he or she has a vocation frequently experiences fear and awe—sometimes even doubt and terror—and yet it is also true that the discovery of one's vocation always brings with it a feeling of joy.

The most beautiful moment, though, is not when we discover God's call, but when we say our "yes," when we act upon God's call, when we unite our will to his will.

This act of uniting our will to God's must last our whole life long; it is a continual "yes" which we must say to God as he repeats his "yes" for all eternity.

Once we have discovered our vocation we understand better why God asks us to give up everything else. The expression "give up" might seem negative, but it is actually not so much a matter of giving something up, as of acquiring the many gifts which God has prepared for us.

In a vocation, renunciation is like the other side of the coin. It is summed up in various passages in Luke's Gospel.

> As they were making their way along, someone said to him, "I will be your follower wherever you go." Jesus said to him, "The foxes have lairs, the birds of the sky have nests, but the Son of Man has nowhere to lay his head" (Lk. 9:57-58).

Here we see someone who has been following Jesus, who is fascinated by him, and who perhaps has felt a vocation—a call. However he has not understood the full meaning of this call. And so Jesus—full of love—wants to explain it to him; and says those now well-known words: "Foxes have lairs, the birds of the sky have nests, but the Son of Man has nowhere to lay his head."

To have understood Jesus' call is to have also understood that this call is not an invitation to a life of comfort and security. This is true of every vocation in the Church.

Someone could say, "I feel a vocation," when in fact what he or she actually feels is more an attraction to the externals of the priestly or religious life than to the substance of the vocation itself. Such a person has seen only the marginal aspects of God's call. For instance, one might look at the priesthood and see not only service to God, but also the parish structure, a career—coupled with at least a certain amount of financial security—or, at any rate, a whole set of human trappings. But Jesus speaks clearly to all those who, down through the centuries, will want to follow him: "The Son of Man has nowhere to lay his head."

The vocation is a personal call from Jesus, not from an organization. It is a personal matter between Jesus and the individual, not between the individual and an organization.

Those of you, for example, who truly have a vocation to the focolare,* do not have a vocation to the focolare, but to Jesus. Your vocation will be

---

*A community of consecrated men or women within the Focolare Movement.

THE CALL TO FOLLOW JESUS 91

lived out, in this case, in the focolare; but your vocation is to follow Jesus. Everything else is secondary. You may have a place to live or you may not. You may live out your vocation travelling constantly, as Jesus did, sleeping one night here, another there. Or you may live it out by spending your whole life in the same place. These are all marginal details which have very little to do with the essence of a vocation. What is essential is a desire to follow Jesus and a willingness to regard everything else as unimportant. This means that for someone who follows Jesus the whole world is home. One who decides to follow Jesus cannot say: "I want to follow Jesus, but only in this country or that." Whoever follows Jesus is following the creator of the universe, so he or she is equally at home in Argentina, Hawaii, the Sahara, or the Caucasus.

There is no *place* where it is easier to fulfill one's vocation; a vocation is fulfilled in God. All the surrounding circumstances are secondary—useful because we must live in this world, but worthwhile only to the extent that they are useful. This is the attitude that Jesus asks us to have.

> To another he said, "Come after me." The man replied, "Let me bury my father first." Jesus said to him, "Let the dead bury their dead; come away and proclaim the kingdom of God" (Lk. 9:59-60).

Here Jesus is very clear in specifying what must be one's relationship with one's relatives. In Genesis, after creating woman, God said: "This is why a man leaves his father and mother and joins himself to his wife, and they become one body" (Gen. 2:24 JER). This leaving of one's own family in order to create a new family is considered perfectly normal on a natural level. But in an even deeper and more beautiful fashion the same thing must take place in the case of a vocation, because if we have understood the profound meaning of this call we realize that it is like a spiritual marriage between the soul and Jesus, between the soul and God.

Marriage is the best human term of comparison we have to help us understand the greatness of a vocation. It is obvious that if a person is married, he or she has left everything. So if someone called by God were to reply: "First I'll wait until my father dies," as this disciple did, that person would be demonstrating that he or she has not fully understood what a vocation is all about.

Jesus sees in this disciple a lack of that vibrant and exclusive love which is necessary in one who has a vocation, and so he replies, "Let the dead bury their dead." That is, "Let those who do not live this divine life carry out those tasks. It is not necessary that they be performed by you, since you must proclaim the kingdom of God. You are alive with the true life, and you must spread this life. The things of this world, even the holiest and most beautiful—such as staying with one's family—can be done by others."

Yet another said to him, "I will be your follower, Lord, but first let me take leave of my people at home." Jesus answered him, "Whoever puts his hand to the plow but keeps looking back is unfit for the reign of God" (Lk. 9:61-62).

In this reply, Jesus specifies another essential aspect of a vocation: its perpetuity. It is awe-inspiring to think of God's love. He loves us from all eternity. We cannot merely love him for a few months or a few years. If God gives himself to us totally, we must give ourselves totally to him. If someone is willing to completely give up family and possessions for God, but only for a time, then he or she is not fit for the kingdom of heaven.

The Church has made this act of giving sacred by the use of vows—first temporary, then perpetual—which are the outward expression of the act that is taking place in the depths of the person's soul. The fact that we may take vows but may also choose to not take them for a time, or that the Church may tell us out of prudence to delay taking them in order that we may be sure that we have a vocation, is an expression of the Church's maternal love. But we certainly cannot think that we will begin to follow Jesus only when we have taken perpetual vows! We are following Jesus, we are following God, from the moment we understand that we have a vocation and we consent to give ourselves completely to him.

However, we cannot expect that just because we have made this gift of ourselves, we will automatically become holy or perfect; nor does this gift, this marriage between our soul and God, mean that we will always be up to God's love. On the contrary, after having made this act of love, we may at times experience ups and downs, we may fall, we may betray God. But this does not mean that the call, the vocation, no longer exists. We should always keep in mind Peter's denial.

If the call to follow Jesus is so total that from the very outset it is intended to be perpetual, then its acceptance will necessarily involve the renunciation of loved ones and possessions. But God, for his part, will shower us with an abundance of graces and gifts.

It is inconceivable that once God has given himself to a person, and the person has given himself or herself to God, everything should remain as it was before! No. Everything changes. We see this expressed in Jesus' words to his disciples: "You are the salt of the earth. You are the light of the world" (Mt. 5:13,14). We are the light of the world not because we preach or give witness, but because the divine light has been transfused into us, because we belong to God, because we are children of the Light. We are disciples of Jesus, we belong to him; and he is the Light of the world.

When Peter saw the rich young man walk away, he turned to Jesus and asked, "What about us? We have left everything and followed you. What are we to have, then?" Jesus said to him, "Everyone who has left houses, brothers, sisters, father, mother, children or land for the sake of my name will be repaid a hundred times over, and also inherit eternal life" (Mt. 19:27,29 JER).

A person who gives himself or herself to God and renounces everything else experiences a fullness that comes from God and a joy that comes from the knowledge of God's personal love for him or her, a joy that no one else can experience.

This, briefly, is the vocation to follow Jesus, as it is found in the Gospels. But the clearest and most beautiful description of the vocation is still Mark's statement: "Jesus looked at him with love."

8

THE CALL TO DISCIPLESHIP

The Old Testament speaks of a time to come, in which the Lord's disciples will have his law inscribed in their hearts through a special outpouring of the Holy Spirit. On the day of Pentecost, Peter reminds his listeners of this by quoting the prophet Joel (Acts 2:17-21).

The concept of discipleship that emerges from the Scriptures is thus totally different from that held by the secular teachers of the times, for whom a disciple was simply a person who belonged to their school, who had learned their doctrine, and who had become their follower.

Jesus brought about a revolutionary change in both the concept and the reality of discipleship. His disciples are even able to have their Teacher in their hearts. Being a disciple of Jesus, therefore, involves not only a change in one's thinking and one's mentality, but a radical change in oneself: it means becoming a new person. This radical change is brought about by baptism. These new persons are the new disciples foretold in the Old Testament and described in the Gospels.

Here is a passage from Luke in which Jesus explains what he requires of these disciples; that is, of all those who follow him—of all Christians:

> On one occasion when a great crowd was with him, he turned to them and said, "If anyone comes to me without turning his back on his father and mother, his wife and his children, his brothers and sisters, indeed his very self, he cannot be my follower. Anyone who does not take up his cross and follow me cannot be my disciple. If one of you decides to build a tower, will he not first sit down and calculate the outlay to see if he has enough money to complete the project? He will do that for fear of laying the foundation and then not being able to complete the work; for all who saw it would jeer at him, saying, 'that man began to build what he could not finish.'
>
> ". . . In the same way, none of you can be my disciple if he does not renounce all his possessions" (Lk. 14:25-30,33).

Jesus wants to make clear to the great crowd of people who are following him what it means to be his disciple. So he addresses them in these very demanding terms. He demands that his disciples, the ordinary Christians—that is, all of us—put God in first place, above all other affections.

Moreover, he requires that our love for him surpass even our love for ourselves: "Anyone who does not take up his cross and follow me cannot be my disciple."

Jesus also requires us to be detached from our possessions. "None of you can be my disciple if he does not renounce all his possessions." He is not asking, however, that everyone actually give up their possessions. The call to renounce one's possessions concretely is a grace that our Lord reserves for those who understand the beauty of effective poverty and who feel a special calling to live in poverty. Nonetheless, all Christians must be detached from their possessions in order to put them at the service of God. They must administer what they possess in an unselfish way, regarding it not as their own, but as intended for the good of the community and of society as a whole. At the very least, this means giving what is surplus to the poor, and not living a life of luxury.

Jesus asks this of Christians because, since they have become new persons, they ought to act in a completely new way. They will thereby become part of the divine family whose bond with Jesus is stronger than ties of blood.

> He was still addressing the crowds when his mother and his brothers appeared outside to speak with him. Someone said to him, "Your mother and your brothers are standing out there and they wish to speak to you." He said to the one who had told him, "Who is my mother? Who are my brothers?" Then, extending his hand toward his disciples, he said, "These are my

mother and my brothers. Whoever does the will of my heavenly Father is brother and sister and mother to me" (Mt. 12:46-50).

These words do not reflect negatively in any way upon Mary's relationship with Jesus, for she was certainly his disciple to a far greater extent than we are, and thus she was also bound to him in this way far more than we are. However, Jesus uses this opportunity to make absolutely clear that what counts in the kingdom of God is the new kinship acquired through grace.

Let us take our considerations on this a bit further, because it frequently happens in our Christian life that we put the emphasis on things which are of very little importance, or we stress certain religious practices which of themselves are not enough to make one a true Christian.

God is undoubtedly pleased by outward religious observances; but if Jesus were to come on earth today, perhaps he would tell us that to have taken on the outward appearances of Christianity while inwardly remaining substantially the same worldly people as before, is not Christianity at all; it is only a semblance of Christianity.

Jesus dared to tell us, "Love your enemies, do good to those who hate you. . . . If you love those who love you, what credit is that to you? Even sinners love those who love them. . . . Love your enemy and do good" (Lk. 6:27,32,35). But I wonder how many of us Christians love those who maltreat us. Jesus could say to those of us who do not, "You are like the pagans. You are still pagans in spirit, even if you go to Church on Sunday, even if outwardly you observe other religious practices."

See how important it is, therefore, to have the new spirit that the Gospel invites us all to have, since a total love for God is required of all Christians, and not just a few. To live in this spirit is not something heroic, it is what every ordinary Christian ought to do.

We might wonder why many do not live their Christianity in this total way. Perhaps they have not yet become aware that God is calling them to do so. In contrast, however, there are many others in the Church who have given and are continuing to give a beautiful example in this regard.

If we do not wish to stop at the bare minimum, it is obvious that we must do at least what is required of Christians in general; that is, give God the first place in our lives and be detached from everything—career, reputation, family, possessions, the comforts of life. This is the basis for everything else.

We know that from among his disciples Jesus chose the Twelve and consecrated them in a special way, giving them the episcopal, apostolic charism to be the founders of the Church and the ones who would pass on the Gospel message.

THE CALL TO DISCIPLESHIP 101

But the Gospel also mentions another group of disciples: the seventy-two. I think that all of us can take these seventy-two as an example to follow. We know that they were disciples of Jesus—that is, persons who wanted to live the new spirit of the Gospel, to be filled with God and detached from everything else. They wanted to belong to the new family of Jesus, and in addition they were ready to collaborate with him by taking an active part in the spreading of the kingdom of God. Scripture does not say that the seventy-two were priests; they were ordinary disciples whom Jesus used to spread the kingdom of God. I would like to meditate with you now on the one passage in Scripture that speaks of them.

"After this, the Lord appointed a further seventy-two and sent them in pairs before him to every town and place he intended to visit" (Lk. 10:1). We see immediately that these seventy-two have a mission: to prepare the way for Jesus. He sends them two by two, so that they can encourage and support one another in their witness to the Gospel, and so that they may experience the efficacy of his words, "Where two or three are gathered in my name, there am I in their midst" (Mt. 18:20).

"He said to them: 'The harvest is rich but the workers are few; therefore ask the harvest-master to send workers to his harvest'" (Lk. 10:2). This passage is found in both Luke and Matthew (9:37). It is one of the most mysterious of Jesus' statements because it shows that he—who is God and is almighty, the redeemer of the human race—is mindful of all those of good will, and though he could convert them directly, he wills to bring about the conversion of humanity through human intermediaries. He wants persons who will act as intermediaries between himself and those who are waiting for him.

At that moment Jesus is sad. He sees that the harvest is abundant, that many people are ready. And he himself is ready. But the intermediaries are missing. He has the power to raise up these intermediaries himself, to create them from the very stones of the ground, but he wills that even these intermediaries be raised up as a result of the prayers of other intermediaries.

God wants to leave us all free, and he has willed to make the salvation of the human race dependent on our personal cooperation with his grace.

This is at once profound and awe-inspiring, and it ought to make us stop and think. God will raise up apostolic persons only if I pray, and he links the conversion of others to my prayer and intercession. God—who can do anything, who could convert everyone in an instant, who with a single divine grace could enlighten everyone—this God has willed that in heaven we might be able to hear him say to us, "See, you have helped me in the redemption of the world. You have shared my passion and my victory."

THE CALL TO DISCIPLESHIP 103

In some way the number of present-day apostles depends upon us; it is linked to our prayers. God needs us—he *wills* to have need of us. But he does not need our human activism. We must keep this in mind, lest we throw ourselves into all kinds of purely human activities, only to find that they do not produce any fruitful results. (Hence, for example, to intercede on behalf of those whom we believe God may be calling does not mean to annoy them with our insistence or to put pressure on them.) It will be as a result of our prayers, that God will give those he has called to be apostles the grace to understand their apostolic mission. It is a matter of doing our part so that God can speak.

Jesus sees the seventy-two about to set out on their mission; but he also sees the world, and so he says, "Be on your way, and remember; I am sending you as lambs in the midst of wolves" (Lk. 10:3). Note that he does not say, "I am sending you like hunters in the midst of wolves so that you can capture them." No, our strength in the face of wolves is to be lambs. This is another mystery.

How often we are tempted instead to be wolves with the wolves, to defend the rights of truth by using the same means that others are using to deny it. To do so, however, would be a mistake in judgment, an example of purely human reasoning. It would show that we were not disciples of Jesus. He wants us to be lambs.

Of course, he goes on to tell us that we should be

not only simple as doves but wise as serpents. To be lambs does not mean to be foolhardy. And to be simple and wise means to consider carefully all that is necessary in order to bring the good news, but in a spirit of humility and meekness.

Let us remember, above all, Jesus' words, "Blessed are the meek, for they shall inherit the earth" (Mt. 5:5 RSV). Yes, those who are meek, who make themselves lambs, will render the strong powerless and thus will be able to bring God to everyone and to reign as well—in a spiritual sense, of course; certainly not in the sense of domination or possession.

Still further on, Jesus cautions us about the means to be used in our apostolate: "Carry no purse, no bag, no sandals" (Lk. 10:4 RSV). This is a constant lesson to all of us, for we are frequently concerned about lack of money which we view as an obstacle to the rapid spreading of the kingdom of God. But God's kingdom is not tied to human means. This is not to say that human means are unnecessary, but rather that money is not what brings the kingdom of God. If we bring the kingdom of God in the spirit of poverty, we will also receive whatever money we need.

The more we want to be available in order to bring the kingdom of God, the more we will make ourselves poor. Previously I said that Christ does not ask his disciples to give up their possessions, that it is sufficient if they use and administer them

THE CALL TO DISCIPLESHIP 105

well. This remains true. However, those who retain their possessions will find themselves severely hampered in bringing the kingdom of God. Those who truly want to be apostles, who truly want to bring God's kingdom everywhere, will abandon themselves completely to God and live in evangelical poverty—which does not mean they must live in misery. Whoever does give up everything will receive abundant graces from God; and when such a person attempts to bring God to others, he or she will be a clear channel through which God can pass much more easily.

In other words, we must make full use of human means, but we must not believe that these means are what brings the kingdom of God. The one who brings the kingdom of God is God.

Jesus gives a further instruction, one which was especially applicable to his time and place: "Greet no one along the way" (Lk. 10:4). In Jesus' time, to "greet" someone meant to stop for a while, to have a meal together, to spend the night. In other words, it was a rather lengthy business. Jesus is telling his disciples not to waste time, to stick to the point of their mission, which is to bring the kingdom of God, without stopping to do other things.

He then goes on to say what they should do when they enter someone's home: "On entering any house, first say, 'Peace to this house'" (Lk. 10:5). "Peace to this house" was a usual form of greeting at that time. However, Jesus is not telling his disciples to use it in its usual sense, but in its fullest sense: he is telling them to bring peace—to bring God—to that house.

"If there is a peaceable man there, your peace will rest on him; if not, it will come back to you" (Lk. 10:6). This is also very important, because frequently we are tempted to want to force peace on others, whereas, though we have the obligation to offer God to everyone, we must be detached from the desire to have the other person change his or her way of life. For God has his moment for every person.

We are not supposed to proselytize. We should not and cannot force others to become disciples, nor can we force people to reform their lives.

At times there are persons close to us who cause us to suffer, and frequently it is they we would like to see convert. But God may cause someone else to convert instead. This is because he has particular graces in mind for every person, and he bestows these graces at the right time and in the right moment. Therefore, we must go along with his plan.

God wants to bring his kingdom to others through us, but he is the one who is bringing it and he is the one who prepares people to receive it. We must always be aware that we are nothing, that we are simply God's instruments. It is he who is at work, and he will find the right persons.

If he does not find them, his peace will return to

THE CALL TO DISCIPLESHIP   107

us. We will not have lost anything because of this. We will simply continue on down the road.

"And remain in the same house, eating and drinking what they provide, for the laborer deserves his wages; do not go from house to house" (Lk. 10:7 RSV). Here Jesus indicates that whoever is engaged in the apostolate will receive what he or she needs to live on, as well as the means necessary to carry out the apostolic work itself. However, he cautions the disciples that they must adapt their mentality to the environment in which they find themselves. "Eat and drink what they provide" means that the disciples must try to adapt themselves to the tastes and mentality of the world in which they live. In other words, Jesus is teaching us to "make ourselves one" with those among whom we live and work. He is telling us not to bring our experience, our culture, our mentality, our tastes, but rather to adapt ourselves to what we find. Our aim is to bring God to others; nothing else should interest us.

"Do not go from house to house." This advice is very important when it comes to determining what course we should pursue in our apostolate. It tells us that we must bring the Gospel to others, give it to those who are willing to receive it, and cultivate those who have accepted it. We are not to move from place to place, from one city to another, without ever helping anyone to go into depth spiritually. If we have brought the Gospel to one home, then, by the action of God's grace, his kingdom will spread out from there in various directions, in a mysterious but spontaneous and natural way. We have witnessed this countless times in the spreading of the Movement. Moreover, this is what took place in the first centuries of Christianity.

Jesus cautions that the disciples' preaching should not be a sort of advertising campaign for the Gospel. It should not be simply a compelling proclamation of the Gospel in one home after another, following which the disciples move on to another place. No, if a person accepts the Gospel, then he or she must receive an in-depth follow-up. This is very important if we are to avoid overextending ourselves and if we are to enable those who have accepted the Word of God to persevere.

Jesus continues, "And cure the sick there. Say to them, 'The reign of God is at hand'" (Lk. 10:9). In other words: if there is a need, perform a concrete act of love and then proclaim that the reign of God is at hand.

One must engage in the apostolate motivated by a desire to serve. That is why God gives these disciples the grace to heal the sick. If God does not generally give extraordinary graces like this to us it is because we do not have complete faith in him and we are not living fully in him. If we live completely in Jesus, God will also accomplish extraordinary things through us: extraordinary in that they are

THE CALL TO DISCIPLESHIP 109

true miracles, or extraordinary in the sense that they are exceptional compared to the normal events of everyday life. Jesus is saying here that he will provide special graces to enable us to love others more effectively and thus prepare them to listen to the announcement that the reign of God is near. We can and must love others before we proclaim Christianity to them.

"If the people of any town you enter do not welcome you, go into its streets and say, 'We shake the dust of this town from our feet as testimony against you'" (Lk. 10:10-11). This was a custom of the time, but in this instance it is not a demonstration of contempt but a loving warning, as if to say: "The reign of God is near. Look at the graces you are missing out on!"

Thus it is clear that we must not linger with those who do not want to listen. Just as we are not to convert people forcibly, likewise we are not to waste God's graces or our time on those who will not listen. Once we have proclaimed God's message to them and have warned them that this is a grace from God and that for them to waste it would be a very serious matter, then we must move on to another place or another city, bringing the kingdom of God.

Jesus goes on to say that the graces associated with the Gospel are so great that if the most sinful cities of the ancient world had received these graces, they would certainly have converted.

Then he says, "Anyone who listens to you listens to me; anyone who rejects you rejects me, and those who reject me reject the one who sent me" (Lk. 10:16 JER). This is beautiful! Beautiful and frightening. If we are bearers of the kingdom of God, then whoever welcomes us welcomes God in a very special way. A welcome given to anyone is always a welcome given to God, but whoever welcomes one who is bringing God welcomes Jesus in a special way; and whoever welcomes Jesus welcomes the one who sent him: that is, the Father. Whoever, instead, rejects the apostles, rejects God.

"The seventy-two returned in jubilation saying, 'Master, even the demons are subject to us in your name'" (Lk. 10:17). On occasion, you too have gone to bring God to others, to engage in apostolic activity. And I am certain that you came back rejoicing, saying that you had seen many people touched by God's grace. That is the same thing that the seventy-two tell Jesus when they return to him, as to their father, and tell him about the miracles they have witnessed. And Jesus replies: "I watched Satan fall from the sky like lightning" (Lk. 10:18). I think that this same thing still happens today; that is, the more the kingdom of God spreads, the more the demons flee. And if we were like Jesus we would see it; we would see Satan fleeing.

"Nevertheless," says Jesus, "do not rejoice so much in the fact that the devils are subject to you as that your names are inscribed in heaven" (Lk.

10:20). It is not the apostolate that matters, nor even the fact of having power over demons, but rather that our names be inscribed in heaven, that we be children of God.

"Rejoice that your names are inscribed in heaven" means "Rejoice that you belong to God, that you are his children." In antiquity a name meant everything: it meant the person, or the essence of the thing named. It was the expression of a whole reality. So Jesus is actually saying: "Rejoice that you are in heaven. What counts is that you are part of the kingdom of God."

Seeing around him all these disciples—who are young, or at least young in spirit—"Jesus rejoiced in the Holy Spirit" (Lk. 10:21). This is one of the few passages in the Gospels that reveal Jesus' feelings to us. We see how pleased he is to see the disciples who have returned from bringing the kingdom of God to others. And speaking to the Father, he says: "I offer you praise, O Father, Lord of heaven and earth, because what you have hidden from the learned and the clever you have revealed to the merest children. Yes, Father, you have graciously willed it so" (Lk. 10:21-22).

Jesus looks at the seventy-two: they are not learned, they are not theologians, they are not exceptionally clever, but they have understood the kingdom of God and have taken it to others. And seeing that it has pleased Providence to reveal the plans and the wisdom of God not on the basis of human ability but on the basis of a person's response to grace, Jesus rejoices at this new and just order of things, this overturning of the scale of human values, this new reign that is being established on earth; and he thanks the Father for having hidden these things from the wise and the worldly and having revealed them to mere children.

9

FAITH, HOPE, AND LOVE

If any one of us were asked about original sin, we would surely mention its negative consequences and the harmful effects it has had on our human nature. But what we might not stress enough is the fact that even though we have passions which tend toward evil, human nature was not intrinsically corrupted by original sin.

In the past the term "passions" did not have the same meaning we assign to it today. "Passions" meant the various powers and tendencies of the soul which in themselves are good, but which can become negative.

If we are to understand the true value of the Christian life and of the theological virtues (faith, hope, and love) we must hold that human nature—inasmuch as it has been created by God—is good, even though it has been wounded by original sin.

Since human nature is basically good, the Christian life will bring about the fullest development of all its potential. For the Christian life is a life directed towards God and towards the good of humanity, and this involves the fullest exercise of all our human talents and energies.

The theological virtues of faith, hope, and love are therefore very important because they are the virtues that enable us to live for God and to reach our fullest potential.

We generally think of faith as belief in a statement or creed containing the truths revealed by God; but while this is certainly one aspect of faith, it is not everything. Speaking more of the person doing the believing, we can say that faith is the activity of a human intelligence which has been enriched by the supernatural. It is an intelligence made capable of making contact with God, with the mystery of God.

But faith is not simply an intellectual acceptance of the things of God. It involves looking at the whole world from God's point of view. If, for example, I relate to the persons I meet in a purely human way, then I will see in them nothing more than what I am able to perceive with my human nature. In a wider, Christian view, however—which takes into account the whole human being—I will see these persons as other members of the Mystical Body of Christ; in them I will see Jesus. Therefore, "seeing" Jesus in our neighbor is an act of Christian intelligence.

Another aspect of faith is at work when we use

FAITH, HOPE, AND LOVE 115

our Christian intelligence to see God's will beneath the various circumstances which Providence has disposed in our lives.

If we live in the spirit of faith, with our intelligence thus sharpened, we will feel such a strong affinity between our own intellect and the truths revealed by God that—even though they remain a mystery—they will no longer seem so incomprehensible. They will no longer seem to be truths that must be accepted without any possible explanation whatsoever.

The apostles and the first Christians looked at things in this way. Only later on did the distinction begin to arise between the truths of faith and the spirit of faith: a distinction which led, in many instances, to a separation between the truths which one must believe in order to be saved, and the spirit of faith which enables one to look with a supernatural eye not only at those particular truths but at everything around us.

This is what our present-day Christianity needs: the spirit of faith which enables us to believe in revealed truth and prompts us to apply them to all the circumstances of life. If we do not have this spirit of faith—that is, if we do not "lose" our human intelligence in God, in order to have it returned to us enriched with the supernatural—we will understand very little of the Christian life and we will begin to judge, because we will be looking at divine things from a purely human point of view. In order to have this new, superior intelligence, we must give our natural intelligence to God with love.

The early Christians considered that a person who did not want to lose his or her own intellect in God, was acting like someone who does not reason. In giving our own mind to God, we will certainly experience a bit of darkness, and in that moment we will have to make an act of faith. But if we entrust ourselves to the divine intelligence, we will soon come to share in it in some way.

Thus we will be able to accept the great truths of faith and we will then see Christianity take hold of our whole life: we will be able to see Jesus in others and to see God's will in the circumstances of life.

The spirit of faith, therefore, must constantly grow in us, and we must become ever more capable of seeing things through God's eyes and with his intelligence, so that we may finally have that charismatic faith of which Jesus speaks: "If you had faith the size of a mustard seed, you would be able to say to this mountain, 'Move from here to there,' and it would move" (Mt. 17:20).

Here Jesus is describing what Paul will later define as the charism of faith. This is the faith we must have. When Jesus invited his listeners to have this type of faith, he was not speaking to a select few, but to all Christians. Therefore all Christians can reach the point of having this charismatic faith.

We can acquire charismatic faith through prayer

and by looking at things objectively. In other words, Jesus did not mean that we would be able to move mountains just for the fun of it, but rather that if moving a mountain should be truly useful for the kingdom of God, and if we have faith, then even this miracle will occur.

At times we may hear someone say that in particular mission areas everyone is poor, and therefore it is impossible to bring them Christianity. Such reasoning is entirely human; it is not at all the reasoning of someone who has charismatic faith, because if schools and hospitals are necessary in that area, then God will send them. What we must do is view things with an intelligence that is both human and divine, that has been enlightened and made complete by Christianity.

We may also hear that the people in a particular region are very unreceptive to Christianity. This may well be true; but it is also true that we have probably not made use of all the charismatic possibilities that the Lord has given us.

Every place on earth has its particular "mountains" to be moved, and we must confess that if we are unsuccessful in moving them, the only reason is that we do not have the faith that God is asking of us. It is our own fault if we do not take full advantage of the graces the Lord has given us for the spreading of Christianity.

Finally, some might object that because they personally are not good enough, they cannot have such great faith. Let them recall then, how Jesus addressed the two blind men who came to him wanting to be cured:

> Jesus said to them, "Are you confident I can do this?" "Yes, Lord," they told him. At that he touched their eyes and said, "Because of your faith it shall be done to you"; and they recovered their sight (Mt. 9:28-30).

Let them also remember the dialogue between Jesus and the father of the possessed boy:

> As they approached the disciples, they saw a large crowd standing around, and scribes in lively discussion with them. Immediately on catching sight of Jesus, the whole crowd was overcome with awe. They ran up to greet him. He asked them, "What are you discussing among yourselves?" "Teacher," a man in the crowd replied, "I have brought my son to you because he is possessed by a mute spirit. Whenever it seizes him it throws him down; he foams at the mouth and grinds his teeth and becomes rigid. Just now I asked your disciples to expel him, but they were unable to do so."
> He replied by saying to the crowd, "What an unbelieving lot you are! How long must I remain with you? How long can I endure you? Bring him to me."
> When they did so the spirit caught sight of Jesus and immediately threw the boy into convulsions. As he fell to the ground he began to roll around and foam at the mouth. Then Jesus questioned the father: "How long has this been happening to him?" "From

childhood," the father replied. "Often it throws him into fire and into water. You would think it would kill him. If out of the kindness of your heart you can do anything to help us, please do!" Jesus said, "'If you can'? Everything is possible to a man who trusts." The boy's father immediately exclaimed, "I do believe! Help my lack of trust!" Jesus, on seeing a crowd gathering, reprimanded the unclean spirit by saying to him, "Mute and deaf spirit, I command you: Get out of him and never enter him again!" Shouting, and throwing the boy into convulsions, it came out of him (Mk. 9:14-26).

Jesus asks charismatic faith even of sinners. His question, "Do you believe I can do this?" was addressed not to Peter or to some of his other disciples, but to ordinary people who had turned to him for help.

Therefore he can ask this same faith of us as well, regardless of how little or how much we have progressed in the spiritual life, because at whatever point we are we can always have a rapport with him, we can always ask him for faith.

Another great Christian virtue is hope. Hope is believing in the omnipotence of God, and believing that he will give us the graces necessary to attain salvation. We sin against hope when we believe that God does not want to save us.

Hope is that virtue by which we tend towards God, but with a certain reference to ourselves. This is because, as part of the universe, we belong to God, who has a definite plan for us. Therefore he wants us to have some concern for ourselves. And in this concern for ourselves he wants us to believe that he loves us and that he will save us.

God gives everyone the graces necessary to attain salvation, and all of us can be saved if we want to be. And since all of us want to be saved, hope acquires an element of certainty: the certainty that as long as I desire to be saved, I can be saved.

God's love is so great that even if we did not wish to be saved, he would care for us anyway, trying to save us.

In those who give their lives to God, the virtue of hope must grow and develop, especially after the period of initial graces has passed and our Lord begins to mold them, allowing them to experience trials, temptations and worries.

It is then that hope is put to the test, that our trust in God's personal concern for us is tested. This trust in God must be so strong that it touches our innermost self and gives peace to our soul. If it is merely a generic trust in God which does not involve me, it is not true hope, because it lacks the element of a filial relationship with God. We must have the same sort of relationship with God that a child has with its mother. Children know that their mother will provide whatever they need, and feel peaceful and secure because of the confidence she inspires.

Hope involves abandoning ourselves to God, believing that he loves us so much that we can confidently place ourselves in his hands. Temptations against hope which causes us to lack this trust can slow our Christian life to a virtual standstill.

We must be wary, for example, of mistaking for humility what is actually a lack of trust in God, a lack of the positive virtue of hope. For hope places us in God's hands. It prompts us to give ourselves fully to him, even when we have been in the wrong.

We must trust in God's love for us, even if we have imperfections and faults, because even then God loves us. Naturally he wants us to reform and not to persist in our faults; but above all he wants us to be trusting, like little children who believe in love.

So, whatever might be asked of us for the glory of God, we must remember that we possess within us a potential for Christian life which we must not suffocate, but must continually develop, with the awareness that God is helping us. The virtue of hope gives us peace of mind: I may be the way I am, with all my faults, but God is there and he cares for me, and he will give me all the graces I need to go on.

As we see, hope is an extremely important virtue, because the temptation to lose heart can come to all of us. I believe that many young people set out to live Christian lives, but because they are assailed by temptations and perhaps fall into sin, they conclude that Christianity is impossible to live and so they stop trying and settle for a purely natural life. One cause of this is that they have not been told enough about hope.

Being a Christian does not mean that one is immune from trials and difficulties. The Gospel tells us that Peter denied Jesus. Peter, the one who had been chosen by Jesus to confirm his brothers in their faith, denied him. Just imagine what Peter must have gone through afterwards! But what made him certain that Jesus loved him in spite of it all? Hope.

I think we Christians ought to have a thorough understanding of this virtue which touches our lives so intimately and which continually gives us the opportunity to grow in the spiritual life. How many people would become fervent if only they knew this virtue better!

Finally, let us consider love. The Christian virtue of love of God is the act of total love with which we give ourselves to God.

When we first encountered the spirit of the Gospel, we were attracted by it; and soon we understood that in spite of our limitations we have to love God completely.

The act of love which God asks of us is the complete gift of ourselves: of our will, of our intelligence, of all that we are. This act of love is not simply a feeling of affection towards God, although—since this total gift of ourselves involves all our faculties—it can certainly affect our feelings and may even lead us to feel a strong emotional attraction towards God. But this is secondary and non-essential. Although it may be helpful, it is not what really counts. What counts is the act of love for God, the fundamental act of love which we must make.

All Christians must make this act of love in one form or another. Just as every Christian must have the virtues of faith and hope, so each is asked to make this complete gift of self. It is very important that this be understood, because at times people confuse this act of total giving of oneself to God with the vocation to the religious life.

Everyone must choose to put God at the center of his or her life. This choice is then lived out in a variety of ways. One person will remain at home, another will marry, another will enter a monastery. One will become a priest, another will become committed in a particular sector of secular society. But all of this is secondary. What is necessary is the total act of love of God, which is the fundamental act of the Christian life. And we must renew this act continually; we must constantly remind ourselves that we have given ourselves totally to God.

Since God became incarnate in Jesus, and in so doing united himself mystically to the whole of humanity, our act of total love of God must now become an act of total love toward our neighbor.

It is not so much the various activities we perform which will make us saints, but rather the theological virtue of love, which we put into practice by loving God and by loving one another.

Moreover, the spiritual level of humanity will not be raised so much by our external activities, as by our raising the level of our own individual and collective spiritual lives through living with Jesus in our midst. In this way we will help to elevate the lives of others and we will make our contribution so that God may be universally loved.

10

WISDOM

I would like to read with you what Scripture has to say about the type of knowledge we call wisdom.

Wisdom does not depend on knowledge received through the senses or on knowledge arrived at by mere reasoning. Wisdom causes us to put aside these other types of knowledge in order to reach intellectual contact with Intelligence itself, who is God.

In the Old Testament, wisdom is described in the following terms:

> Wisdom is radiant and unfading,
> and she is easily discerned by those who love her,
> and is found by those who seek her.
> She hastens to make herself known to those who desire her.
> He who rises early to seek her will have no difficulty,
> for he will find her sitting at his gates.
>
> (Wis. 6:12-14)

I would like to point out that all of you are here because you love wisdom, even though in coming to this school* many of you were not consciously aware of your need to acquire it. The very fact that you have come from all over the world shows that Wisdom—who is God—has anticipated your desire and led you here.

> The beginning of wisdom is the most sincere desire for instruction,
> and concern for instruction is love of her,
> and love of her is the keeping of her laws.
> (Wis. 6:17-18)

As you see, in order to acquire wisdom we must indeed develop our intellectual capabilities. But that alone is not enough. If we wish to acquire wisdom we must obey her laws. And this point overturns all the usual methods of instruction.

If we want to have a school which will enable us to attain wisdom, we must create a school where study plays a definite role, but where what really counts is to put into practice the norms of wisdom. Only then shall we be able to attain wisdom.

If, by chance, we wonder whether wisdom was made for us and whether we are capable of acquiring it, or if we think that wisdom is a type of knowledge reserved for great geniuses and that, therefore,

---

*This talk was addressed to the young men and women of the Focolare Movement's international school of spiritual formation at Loppiano, near Florence, Italy.

acquiring it must be very difficult, here is our answer:

> I also am mortal, like all men, a descendant of the first-formed child of earth;
> and in the womb of a mother I was molded into flesh. . . .
> And when I was born I began to breathe the common air,
> and fell upon the kindred earth,
> and my first sound was a cry, like that of all.
> I was nursed with care in swaddling cloths.
> For no king has had a different beginning of existence;
> there is for all mankind one entrance into life, and a common departure.
>
> Therefore I prayed and understanding was given me;
> I called upon God, and the spirit of wisdom came to me.
>
> (Wis. 7:1,3-7)

These words are a great consolation to all of us, because they make it clear that one does not need to have had a special sort of education in order to acquire wisdom. It is enough to be a descendant of Adam. Although we have been fashioned from the earth like all other human beings, we need only ask for wisdom in order to obtain it.

Therefore all of us can possess it; we do not need special intelligence. We must, however, make a choice:

> I preferred her to scepters and thrones,
> and I accounted wealth as nothing in comparison
> with her.
> Neither did I liken to her any priceless gem,
> because all gold is but a little sand in her sight,
> and silver will be accounted as clay before her.
> I loved her more than health and beauty,
> and I chose to have her rather than light.
>
> (Wis. 7:8-10)

It is absolutely essential, therefore, to give God the first place in our lives, to put him before everything else. In our own case, this means to be detached from all this world's goods, to love our neighbor, to live a communitarian spiritual life, and to overcome the various discomforts associated with this new school.

Someone might think that if in this school of yours all your time could be dedicated to scholarship, without the need to go and search for work in the city, you would get more out of it. But this is not so, because wisdom can be acquired only in the midst of all the down-to-earth difficulties that normal life entails. Furthermore, shoulder to shoulder with other factory and office workers, we learn much more about certain values of human life than any book could ever tell us.

As you work you will learn many extremely important things, and you will realize that academic studies are not the only important thing in life.

If in every moment—whether you are studying or serving your neighbor—you give of yourself in the spirit of the Gospel, then God will be able to give you his wisdom.

> All good things came to me along with her,
> and in her hands uncounted wealth.
> I rejoiced in them all, because wisdom leads them;
> but I did not know that she was their mother.
> (Wis. 7:11-12)

God does not ask everything of us in order that he might give us wisdom only; he also gives us everything we need in life. But these goods will be a fruit of wisdom, a consequence of the fact that we have loved and chosen God. Notice how one who possesses wisdom acts:

> I learned without guile and I impart without grudging;
> I do not hide her wealth,
> for it is an unfailing treasure for men;
> those who get it obtain friendship with God,
> commended for the gifts that come from instruction.
> (Wis. 7:13-14)

Scripture goes on to describe other qualities of wisdom. Wisdom not only brings with it the good things of this earth, but it gives us a true understanding of the world around us, an understanding that others must work a lifetime to acquire. To have attained wisdom is to have come to a fuller knowledge of the natural worth of things.

> For it is [God] who gave me unerring knowledge of what exists,
> to know the structure of the world and the activity of the elements;
> the beginning and end and middle of times,
> the alternation of the solstices and the changes of the seasons,
> the cycles of the years and the constellations of the stars,
> the natures of animals and the tempers of wild beasts,
> the powers of spirits and the reasonings of men,
> the varieties of plants and the virtues of roots.
> (Wis. 7:17-20)

The light of wisdom is so strong that it enables us to understand the things of this earth in every aspect.

From the little I have said, we can readily see that to speak of wisdom is to speak of God—God who enlightens us in such a profound way. Therefore, in order to describe wisdom the sacred writer has been forced to use many adjectives. Through them, or rather through an intuition that transcends their literal meaning, we are able to glimpse what wisdom is.

For in her there is a spirit that is intelligent, holy,
unique, manifold, subtle,
mobile, clear, unpolluted,
distinct, invulnerable, loving the good, keen,
irresistible, beneficent, humane,
steadfast, sure, free from anxiety,
all-powerful, overseeing all,
and penetrating through all spirits
that are intelligent and pure and most subtle.
For wisdom is more mobile than any motion;
because of her pureness she pervades and penetrates
  all things.
For she is a breath of the power of God,
and a pure emanation of the glory of the Almighty;
therefore nothing defiled gains entrance into her.
For she is a reflection of eternal light,
a spotless mirror of the working of God,
and an image of his goodness.
Though she is but one, she can do all things,
and while remaining in herself, she renews all
  things;
in every generation she passes into holy souls
and makes them friends of God and prophets;
for God loves nothing so much as the man who
  lives with wisdom.
For she is more beautiful than the sun.

(Wis. 7:22-29)

Having given us this marvelous description of wisdom, Scripture tells us what we must do once we have glimpsed wisdom, once we have understood what it is:

> I loved her and sought her from my youth,
> and I desired to take her for my bride,
> and I became enamored of her beauty.
>
> (Wis. 8:2)

Here at this school, once we have advanced beyond first impressions and have understood that Wisdom—God—is behind the life here, we feel the desire to give ourselves completely to God, to espouse him and to espouse wisdom.

And this is the most important thing that this school can do: lead our soul and our intellect to live always with wisdom.

However, this involves a step that each of us must take personally. For the discovery of God is a personal experience; and to resolve to stay always with him is a personal act. This school ought to prepare you to discover wisdom and to discover God and to love him totally.

Scripture tells us not that we should love wisdom for a year or two, but that we must take wisdom as our spouse. This expression indicates that God must receive all our love and that this love must last forever; it must be total in every way.

Once we have embraced wisdom, "she teaches self-control and prudence, justice and courage; nothing in life is more profitable to men than these" (Wis. 8:7). The discovery of God and of wisdom also brings with it other natural human virtues that are aroused and developed in us by wisdom itself.

A person who embraces wisdom and embraces God changes completely, and everyone else around senses that he or she is no longer the same person as before.

> Because of her I shall have glory among the multitudes
> and honor in the presence of the elders, though I am young.
> I shall be found keen in judgment,
> and in the sight of rulers I shall be admired.
> When I am silent they will wait for me,
> and when I speak they will give heed;
> and when I speak at greater length they will put their hands on their mouths.
> Because of her I shall have immortality,
> and leave an everlasting remembrance to those who come after me.
>
> (Wis. 8:10-13)

The primary goal of our Christian education, therefore, should be the attainment of wisdom.

11

REACHING FOR MORE

I would like to outline for you the various stages in the spiritual ascent to God of the Christian who lives an active life of apostolate. Though this will be only a rough sketch, perhaps it will assist us in our own journey toward God by pointing out the difficulties that have to be overcome and helping us to recognize that all the trials God sends or permits are intended to help us progress in the spiritual life.

Naturally, what I am going to say will not actually occur in such a systematic fashion; nor will every detail mentioned necessarily be present in every individual's life.

Once we have understood the essence of Christianity and have reoriented our lives toward God, we see that everything is "vanity of vanities" (Eccl. 1:2) and put God at the first place in our lives. At this point, we have made what might be referred to as a first choice of God. A phase of the spiritual life then begins which is known as the active purification of the senses.

In the initial stages of the spiritual life one can easily see that God disposes circumstances in such a way as to oblige us to undergo a certain purification. All of us are basically inclined to seek pleasure in the delight of our senses. By enkindling the flame of love in our souls, God gives us the opportunity to mortify our senses.

In every phase of the spiritual life, mortification is important. However, in a life of apostolate it is not so much mortification sought after as such, but rather mortification brought about by circumstances, or suggested by our love for our neighbor.

Love of neighbor motivates us to help others, to bear with them, to care for them; and this implies mortifying ourselves.

Since these acts of mortification are motivated by love, we may not look upon them or the suffering they involve as mortification. But this does not mean that for that reason they are less meritorious. The contrary is true: the more love there is in an action, the more meritorious it is, even though love has made it less of a burden.

The way to God is indeed paved with acts of mortification and penance—but penances which result from acts of self-giving and love for others.

In this, as in all the stages of the spiritual life, it is important to live the present moment intensely in order to concentrate our will on what we are doing, forgetting the past.

This period of the spiritual life is marked by a firm decision to want to love God and neighbor with our whole heart, mind and strength, to give ourselves completely, insofar as we are able. If we do this all day, giving of ourselves from morning till evening, then when the moment comes to recollect ourselves and to be alone with Jesus we will experience an easy intimacy with him because we will have been with him throughout the day in giving ourselves totally to our neighbor.

This period is characterized by enthusiasm and joy and—as far as I can see—by the absence of any significant trials. Whatever small trials there are are quickly resolved. It almost seems as if one's entire past life has been left behind and completely forgotten, and its temptations are only a distant memory. There are so few temptations it almost seems as if one has reached a state of perpetual peace.

During this initial stage of the spiritual life our Lord exercises a very strong influence over our senses, drawing them to him so that we will use them for him.

Following this period—which may be quite prolonged—there comes a time when we no longer *feel* the influence of these graces which God has been giving us to help us in our conversion. The reality, however, is not that our Lord is withdrawing his grace, but that he is calling us to give of ourselves more fully. And so the attractions to the interior life, which previously had been able to captivate our senses, no longer have the power to arouse that same enthusiastic self-giving that we formerly experienced. A deeper and purer love for God must now direct and sustain our gift of self.

In Jesus crucified and forsaken, whom we now begin to understand a little better, we can find the strength to overcome these first difficulties.

God wants to purify our soul in a deeper way, and so during this period of the spiritual life we begin to experience trials in the form of worries and scruples about our past life, as well as temptations so strong that we are not sure whether they are sins or merely temptations. We may also experience doubts of faith. These doubts come especially to persons who have previously had their own rationalistic way of thinking, which they must now lose. In fact, the trials that we experience at this time generally correspond closely to the defects of our past life. Previously, we had fallen into bad habits, and now these come to the surface again in order to be purified and eliminated.

The purification we are speaking of is not yet anything on a large scale, but merely a first attempt at tidying things up, a scraping away of the built-up grime in order to get on with the spiritual life.

Nonetheless, at this stage one does experience moments of suffering, and these are felt all the more since they are the first truly spiritual sufferings we have experienced. Moreover, since we are still inexperienced in the spiritual life and our union with God is just beginning, our soul experiences great confusion and we think that we have gone backwards.

Experts on the spiritual life explain that this suffering is the result of a new light from God which illuminates the soul and enables us to see ourselves in a completely different way. In other words these trials are directly related to God's presence in the soul and to the fact that he has begun to work in us and to enter more deeply into our being.

There are two dangers characteristic of this stage of the spiritual life. The first is that of thinking: "I used to be so well off; but now that I have begun to love God with all my heart and soul, I am in torment. This must mean that such a life is impossible, that I have set my spiritual life on the wrong course, that things were better before. . . ." In other words, we can become disheartened and this can have very harmful effects. For if we are overwhelmed by depression for this or other reasons, we become much more vulnerable to the temptation to fall back into sin—not because the allurements to sin are any stronger, but because of our own weakened spiritual condition. When a person is spiritually exhausted, drained, worn out, and has almost no strength left to fight back and resist temptation, the devil can easily cause him or her to fall.

At the opposite end of the spectrum lies the second danger: the tendency to brush problems aside in order not to have to face them. Persons who succumb to this danger, instead of taking up their cross throw it away, thus wasting their suffering. Such persons become not scrupulous but lax, viewing everything in a simplistic fashion, not because they were unable to sense the purification in their lives, but because when they felt it coming they did not have the courage to face it and accept it. Perhaps such persons may never do anything evil, but they will always remain superficial.

The only real way to resolve the various difficulties of this period is to love Jesus crucified and forsaken and to love our neighbors, giving of ourselves in each present moment.

Whereas in the beginning love of neighbor brought with it mortification, in this subsequent stage love of neighbor carries us beyond the suffering we feel in our soul, enabling us to find God in our relationships with others.

Therefore, love of neighbor and unity with others is the way to overcome these trials, which God sends us precisely because he wants us to go beyond ourselves, our sufferings, and our weaknesses. The way to accomplish this, however, is not to focus our attention on ourselves (it is enough simply to open our soul to our confessor) but rather to give of ourselves to others, because in them we find Jesus. Others should not even notice what is happening in our soul.

When God has succeeded in his intended purpose and the soul, previously coarse, has become more sensitive to the supernatural, then he causes these trials to vanish, perhaps as the result of something as simple as a few words from one's confessor.

Now the soul enters a new phase and we ask ourselves why we ever had those problems we previously experienced. And we are not even aware of exactly when or how they disappeared because we are now in a totally new stage of the spiritual life.

Having become more sensitive to the voice of God, we begin to give of ourselves much more than before. It is a time of untiring activity when around us others are converted or entire Christian communities come to life. In addition, there are countless spiritual fruits which give glory to God.

By now the soul has indeed grown and advanced in the spiritual life. Simultaneously, however, many traits in the soul, which previously went unnoticed, have also developed and become prominent, threatening to become obstacles to the soul's union with God and love of neighbor. Thus Jesus, like a gardener, must prune the soul, which, like a spiritual plant, has begun to bear fruit.

The need for this pruning derives from the fact that God is not the sole reason behind everything we do. At this point in the spiritual life we give of ourselves wholeheartedly and, in fact, would be unable to give more or act otherwise, as if we were on some other spiritual level. Nevertheless the human element is still present.

And so trials arise which seem to be typical of this period.

REACHING FOR MORE 141

A first trial, and one which causes much suffering, comes from a lack of understanding on the part of those among whom we carry out our apostolic activity. We suffer because we have tried to love these people with all our heart, soul, and strength, and we cannot understand how they whom we have helped so much and have taken such an interest in could now deliberately or even unintentionally criticize us. This sort of suffering could provoke a harsh reaction on our part; but this would be very harmful.

When we become the object of criticism, there is a danger that, instead of acknowledging that our actions have really been a mixture of love and selfishness, we ourselves may begin to criticize. We may be tempted to withdraw into ourselves, to rebel, to refuse to have anything more to do with those people, to give up. And these temptations may slow the pace of our spiritual life.

But God permits all these things for our good and to make us progress spiritually.

Another trial may come from the fact that although we have given ourselves extensively to others no visible fruits are forthcoming. Our way of speaking still has so little of God in it that it affects others only superficially. Or so it seems. And thus there is a risk that we may become discouraged or lay the blame on external circumstances or existing difficulties.

During this period, yet another trial may arise due to our impression that our superiors do not appreciate all the good we have done and are doing. This suffering, too, stems from the fact that there is still a certain amount of self love attached to the good that we are actually doing.

To sum up: in all these situations there has been a true giving of self and a real accomplishment of good. But God wants to bring our soul to a higher spiritual plane. He wants us to move beyond our desire to do things, so that we will discover that there is another world that lies beyond the world of activism. At this point we must be open to receive these truly wonderful graces which God is sending us. Otherwise we may remain in this spiritual state for years. These graces must be welcomed, because the trials I have just mentioned come only after one has already worked for God, not when one has done nothing. God cannot ask anything of one who has done nothing.

If we overcome these difficulties, we begin to realize that God has called us to experience a rapport of greater unity with him. And we discover that what the others had been telling us was not mistaken after all, and that it has helped to purify us of the human elements in our apostolate.

Thus, even at this stage of the spiritual life, we find that the purification we need still comes to us as an effect of our unity with others.

At the start, in loving our neighbor we find the mortification we need. Then, later on, our love of neighbor enables us to overcome our first interior trials. And finally, the truth expressed by our brothers and sisters in faith purifies us of those defects which we are unaware of or which we would have never even imagined we had.

This last experience is very important at this point in the spiritual life, especially for someone who is bursting with ideas and initiative, who would like to do "who knows what." Having to listen to others and to put their ideas ahead of one's own is a good purification of the mind, the will, and the heart.

Thus, unity with our neighbor offers us the best opportunity for purification, purification such as we alone would never be able to achieve as quickly.

If we are truly aware that in those who tell us the truth about our faults Jesus is present purifying us, and if we recognize that what the others say is true, even though it is painful, then the truth will make us free and the faults themselves will disappear.

Therefore we must succeed in establishing a fraternal unity with others even when we hear ourselves criticized and judged by them. If, by chance, something of what the others think about us is inexact, it will fade from their minds of itself, because in the light of love and fraternal unity it becomes clear that only what is in conformity with the truth of Jesus is alive and real.

Here we see, as always, that the best course to follow is to love our neighbor.

The times when we do not feel understood by

others are the times we must love them most, because they are able to see in us the faults that we do not see. It is pointless to feel that we are misunderstood, for through others God speaks to us and admonishes us. It is in unity with our neighbor and with all our brothers and sisters in faith, that we are able to see things objectively and to discover our true selves as God wants us to be.

Otherwise there is a risk that we may become isolated, creating a world for ourselves in which we find a certain degree of unity with God and a certain unity with a select circle of people who "support" us and "understand" us.

We must be wary, for although a soul experiences these trials when it is already advanced in the spiritual life, it can still succumb to the temptation to come to a standstill.

The more intimate our unity with God, the more we will be united with our neighbor. If our "unity" with God isolates us from our neighbor, we are certainly not living an authentic spiritual life.

Once again I emphasize that the best course of action in every phase of the spiritual life is: love our neighbor, maintain the presence of Jesus in our midst, live the present moment, and love the cross.

Once a person has progressed beyond the stages of the spiritual life I have briefly mentioned, the soul is much more sensitive and refined. Consequently, the person's apostolate bears much fruit and there is a great flowering of supernatural life

REACHING FOR MORE 145

around him or her. At times even a simple word or greeting from such a person is enough to cause others to sense the presence of the divine in the world.

Even at this point, trials are not lacking, but by now the soul has truly begun to forget itself because it is completely caught up in the divine life and in love of neighbor in the apostolate. Purifications are no longer brought on by faults but by the fact that God wants the soul to be detached from all that it does.

Having reached this level of spiritual maturity, the soul now understands that God alone is truly important and that everything else is of no account: whether one is mistreated or not, whether one is sick or healthy, whether one is able to work or not, whether what one does is interpreted favorably or unfavorably.

Nothing matters to the person at this point except what gives glory to God. Therefore the person loves, independently of what may or may not happen, concerned only with loving God and giving him glory.

Now, having passed this milestone, after all the years of preparation, one begins to live the spiritual life in its fullness.

Even though we will never be able to reach the point when every action will be an act of pure love, nevertheless, the desire to love can still become the prevailing and dominant factor in our actions.

Here, as before, everything is linked to love of

neighbor and to a life of unity with others. And the more we progress in our relationship with God, the more our love and our concern for the problems of humanity will grow and become more universal. The Church's problems will become our problems, not because of an effort of the will but because, being one with the Church, we will feel the sufferings of the Church as our own. And we will see the Church not as a purely external organization, but as humanity regenerated by baptism and already embracing—if only by desire—every human being.

Thus it is that many saints have identified themselves with the problems of their time and place and have given solutions which were both spiritual and social.

We, too, feel more and more closely linked with the whole of humanity as we become more and more deeply engrafted into Christ, who is the alpha and omega, the beginning and end of our spiritual life.

12

PRAYER

"The heavens declare the glory of God" (Ps. 19:2 NAB).

The stars and the planets, by their very presence in the sky, by their blind yet faithful obedience to the orderly laws which govern them, give witness to their Creator and, in a way, acknowledge their relationship to him as his creatures. In their own way, they are praying. It is the same with the creatures such as plants and animals, which are alive but irrational: they express their unconcious prayer by following the laws that govern them.

In our case, since as human beings we are both intelligent and spiritual, this relationship must become a conscious rapport. In us, the acknowledgment of the laws of our nature leads to the discovery of the Creator himself; and the loving and thankful rapport with him—which wells up from our very existence—is prayer. If we go to the root of our being we sense a profound primordial rapport with God, who has brought us into existence and continually sustains us lest we cease to exist.

The fact that our existence depends on God leads us to acknowledge him. But the effects of original sin continually disturb and distract us, causing not only spiritual discomfort but psychological uneasiness, since the whole of our human nature needs to feel in its right relationship with God in order to find its proper balance in the harmony of the universe.

The effects of Adam's sin continually draw us away from living immersed in a constant rapport with God. It is precisely for this reason that prayers are necessary: that is, particular words and actions through which, at particular times, we try to re-establish and to express that interrupted conversation between creature and Creator.

It is evident, though, that these prayers, however indispensable they may be, are worthwhile only as a means for reaching prayer itself. Pious practices are useful only insofar as they open the door to true piety.

Therefore we must always keep in mind that there is a basic difference between external acts, whether vocal or mental, and prayer.

This distinction explains why we may pray even with lengthy prayers, and yet be soundly rebuked: "In your prayer do not rattle on like the pagans. They think they will win a hearing by the sheer multiplication of words. Do not imitate them" (Mt. 6:7-8).

It is interesting to note that the "daily bread" we ask for in the *Our Father* has been interpreted by some to mean prayer itself. In other words, ". . . give us each day our rapport with you."

It is this rapport with God which we must seek and find each day.

Let us now consider how one can find this contact with God in various situations.

For example, a person who is suffering physically or who is so tired or so exhausted that he or she cannot even think—much less go to church—may be quite unable to do any of those things which we normally think are necessary in order to pray. Yet this same person, in a single instant, can offer God his or her whole existence, the entire day and all its suffering. This is one of the most profound forms of prayer, because the individual offers himself or herself completely to God, and thus exhibits the exact attitude one must have in order to find a rapport with him. Yet he or she has not performed any of the external practices which we call prayers.

Another very important form of prayer is accessible to people who are working. I am thinking particularly of factory workers and all those persons who during the day are overwhelmed by such fatigue that they are almost deprived of the ability to think and, therefore, in a sense, of the ability to pray. If in the morning these persons make the simple intention of offering their daily existence to

God, then throughout the whole day they will be living in a profound rapport with him. And I am sure that when evening comes, if these tired workers are able to recollect themselves with God for even a few moments, they will find unity with him, because they will have lived their workday in rapport with him. And that is precisely what is important: to have the right rapport with God.

The whole universe and all human activity can be understood in this way and thus be transformed into one great prayer which the world lifts up to God. All things considered, this is precisely what people today are ready to hear. And yet it is seldom understood, because people think that prayer consists only in certain formulas or external practices that for various reasons not all people are in a position to perform.

Those who have consecrated their lives to God are generally able to dedicate some time during the day to prayers. However, even these prayers can remain something purely external, and therefore an authentic rapport with God is decisive and fundamental. Jesus tells us: "It is not those who say to me, 'Lord, Lord,' who will enter the kingdom of heaven, but the person who does the will of my Father in heaven" (Mt. 7:21 JER).

As for those who are constantly with others all day long, if they maintain a loving and giving attitude, then substantially—even if not explicity—they are in contact with God, because Jesus identifies himself mystically with our neighbor: "In so far as you did this to one of the least of these brothers of mine, you did it to me" (Mt. 25:40 JER).

A rapport of true Christian love with our neighbor is implicity already a prayer.

When this rapport becomes reciprocal, then Jesus is present in our midst, and our implicit prayer becomes increasingly conscious and explicit as our spiritual sensibilities are rendered more refined and more supernatural by this rapport of mutual love.

In the family of Jesus, Mary, and Joseph at Nazareth this prayer in the midst of daily life reached its apex. We must draw ever closer to this model, even though it will always remain an unreachable goal. This prayer is like the experience of the disciples of Emmaus, who spoke with Jesus and whose hearts were inflamed as he taught them, even though they were not fully aware of what was happening. Yes, Jesus has promised to be spiritually present whenever people gather together in mutual Christian love.

Finally, let us speak about prayers. By God's grace, we have the good fortune to be able to strengthen our rapport with him daily, by taking advantage of the many possibilities his love offers us in the liturgy, in meditation, in vocal prayer, and in our visits to Jesus in the Eucharist.

The essential characteristic of liturgical prayer is that it is an act of the Church; therefore it is a communitarian prayer. In liturgy we find our rapport with God together with our brothers and sisters in faith. We really ought to let this fact sink in, for otherwise we may frequently run the risk of "having" liturgies instead of praying, and of allowing ceremony to take precedence over this personal and communitarian rapport with God.

Fortunately, however, since in liturgical prayer it is the Church that prays, every liturgy renews the mysterious rapport of Christianized humanity with God, regardless of all our deficiencies.

Nevertheless, if God has created us with an intelligence, a conscience, and human sensibilities, he evidently wants us to use them in praying; that is, he wants us to respond to his love in a human way, not as a flower responds when placed before the altar.

Liturgical prayer is important because of the social dimension of human nature. It is the prayer in which human beings collectively encounter their Creator, who ratifies this prayer with his presence and with the sacrament of the Eucharist that makes us one with him and with one another.

Our rapport with God is also personal; and this is the aspect most evident in meditation. In meditating, we may find spiritual writings helpful, but whatever we do, we must always keep in mind that God is not an abstraction whom we can satisfy by simply following a set of formulas. He loves us and we ought to love him in return by trying to establish a rapport with him. Meditation is an excellent way to reach this rapport.

A meditative rapport with God can be expressed in many different ways. These are described in books of spirituality which illustrate the various methods of mental prayer. The goal of all these methods is a profound personal contact with God. True mental prayer is this: that the living Jesus is present, listening to us and speaking to us. We must therefore learn how to listen to what he tells us. For Jesus speaks, but his words are not always and immediately perceptible to our intelligence. He speaks to us of everything, but especially of himself; and he is God. He also speaks to us of our own little concerns, heals our brokenness, and enables us to understand how to carry out his will in the diverse circumstances of life. In addition, he lets us see that we have been proud, but must now be humble; that we have been attached to persons and things, but must be so no longer. When we are a little worried he tells us by his very presence in our soul to be at peace.

Spiritually unrefined as we are, we are often unable to understand these things because we cannot grasp the mysterious language with which God speaks to us. But gradually we get better at it. We have already experienced many times that when we have had worries or problems to resolve and have gone to him, we have come away at peace. Through his presence, God has mysteriously encouraged and reassured us.

Sometimes we feel crushed beneath the weight of our own faults and failings and the sense of our own sinfulness. This is a common-enough spiritual trial. But if we are able to reestablish contact with God, we are immediately healed.

Think of the simplicity of the sick woman in the Gospel who was able to say what we are frequently incapable of saying: "If I can touch even his clothes, I shall be well again" (Mk: 5:28 JER).

What a wonderful grace it is, when we are worried by spiritual or material problems, to be able to say: "If I can speak with Jesus, if I can 'touch' him, I will be healed." For God heals those who come before him with this faith. And we must not assume that a sinner is incapable of such contact with God, since the Gospel itself gives us many examples.

In his love, God has willed to link many of the graces he wishes to pour out on the world to our mediation; that is, to our intercession, to the fact that in our rapport with him we ask graces for others.

Therefore, he is pleased when we ask him for these graces; and if we are united to him, he grants our request. This type of prayer is called prayer of petition.

We must ask because God wants us to. In this way he shows his love for us as a mother does when she allows her child to help her so that the child may have the joy of having accomplished something.

God also desires our involvement because of the mystery of the Incarnation, so that we might complete with our sufferings what is lacking in the passion of Christ and complete through our prayers and petitions the distribution of the graces necessary for the salvation of the world.

Jesus tells us: "You will receive all that you pray for, provided you have faith" (Mt. 21:22). Frequently we do not receive, because we do not pray. We say prayers, but we do not pray. And this is why we are not able to obtain graces. We are not praying, we are not in contact with God.

Another form of prayer is vocal prayer, exemplified by the recitation of the rosary. For besides praying as a community in liturgical prayer, which expresses the social dimension of our human nature, and besides praying individually as an expression of our human individuality, we must also pray in a way which is more specifically linked to our human body. Therefore the Church strongly recommends vocal prayer.

With its many centuries of experience, the Church knows human nature and knows that no matter how intelligent or learned we human beings may be, we will always need this type of prayer, so that we may truly give praise to God with our whole being and so that in difficult moments we may regain that spiritual intimacy with God which we might otherwise find beyond our reach.

Therefore the recent popes have continued to recommend that most wonderful vocal prayer: the rosary of the Blessed Virgin Mary, in which we simply and affectionately repeat our love for God and his Blessed Mother. Today this prayer is much-needed, even if our present-day intellectualism inclines us to undervalue vocal prayer and to overvalue other forms of prayer.

We must always keep in mind, however, that all forms of prayer are only helps in our journey to God.

If prayer, understood in its deeper sense, becomes a reality in our lives, we will experience a foretaste of heaven here on earth. For heaven is a constant giving of praise, a continual exchange of love, an eternal conversation between us and God. And therein lies our happiness. We can already begin to experience heaven on earth if we immerse ourselves more and more in this mystery that is both human and divine, natural and supernatural: prayer.

Notes

1. "The word used here by the evangelist ordinarily translates the Hebrew root *sn'*, used in the strictly contrastive Semitic sense, where we would say 'not love.' " (J. Lagrange, *Evangile selon S. Luc* [Paris, 1948], p. 409.)
2. Marchal, *Evangile selon S. Luc* (Paris, 1950), p. 185.
3. Allo, *I Epître aux Corinthiens* (Paris, 1959), p. 183.
4. Augustine, *On the Psalms*, 49, 17 (*PL* 36, 576).
5. Augustine, *Sermons*, V, 2 (*PL* 38, 326).
6. J. Villain, *L'insegnamento sociale della chiesa* (Milan, 1957), p. 141. "Social charity also has something to say about the use and destination of private possessions . . . it obliges us, according to the traditional teaching of the Church, to put these possessions at the service of the community." (Constant Van Gestel, O.P., *La dottrina sociale della chiesa* [Rome, 1965], p. 212.)
7. Basil, *Homélies sur la richesse* (Paris, 1935), p. 34. "Do you want to manage your wealth well? Do you want to keep it? Do not hide it but put it in the hands of the poor. For riches are like wild beasts: if closely confined, they flee; if let loose, they remain where they are. Scripture says, 'He has distributed freely, he has given to the poor; his righteousness endures forever' (Ps. 112:9)." (John Chrysostom, *De capto Eutropio*, 3 [*PG* 52, 399].)
8. Leo XIII, *Quod apostolici muneris* (Encyclical Letter on Socialism), 97 (Rome, December 28, 1878).
9. See Ephesians 4: 22-24, Colossians 3: 9-10.

158 REACHING FOR MORE

10. J. De Guilbert, S.J., *Leçons de Théologie spirituelle*, pp. 334-335.
11. "This is why charity is called the form of faith, namely because the act of faith is completed and shaped by charity." (Thomas Aquinas, *Summa Theologiae*, IIa IIae, 4, 3; trans. T.C. O'Brien in Blackfriars edition, vol. 31 (New York-London, 1974), p. 125.
12. *Letter to Diognetus*, V.1—VI.3 (*PG* 2, 1173b-1176c).
13. *Dogmatic Constitution on Divine Revelation*, Art. 12, in *The Documents of Vatican II*, ed. Walter M. Abbott (New York: America Press, 1966), p. 120.
14. *Divine Revelation*, Art. 21, Abbott, p. 125.
15. *Divine Revelation*, Art. 8, Abbott, p. 116.
16. *Divine Revelation*, Art. 21, Abbott, p. 125.
17. *Divine Revelation*, Art. 8, Abbott, p. 116.
18. See H. Denzinger, *Enchiridion Symbolorum*, ed. 35 (1973), #306. Also *PL* 54, 959.
19. *Decree on the Apostolate of the Laity*, Art. 18, Abbott, p. 508.
20. *Constitution on the Sacred Liturgy*, Art. 7, Abbott, p. 141.
21. *Decree on the Appropriate Renewal of the Religious Life*, Art. 15, Abbott, p. 477.
22. *Dogmatic Constitution on the Church*, Ch. 3, Abbott, pp. 37-56.
23. See Ambrose, *On the Psalms*, XLIII, 31. Also *PL* 15, 1929.
24. See Thomas Aquinas, *Summa Theologiae*, III, 50, 6; trans. R.T.A. Murphy in Blackfriars edition, vol. 54 (New York-London, 1965), p. 135.